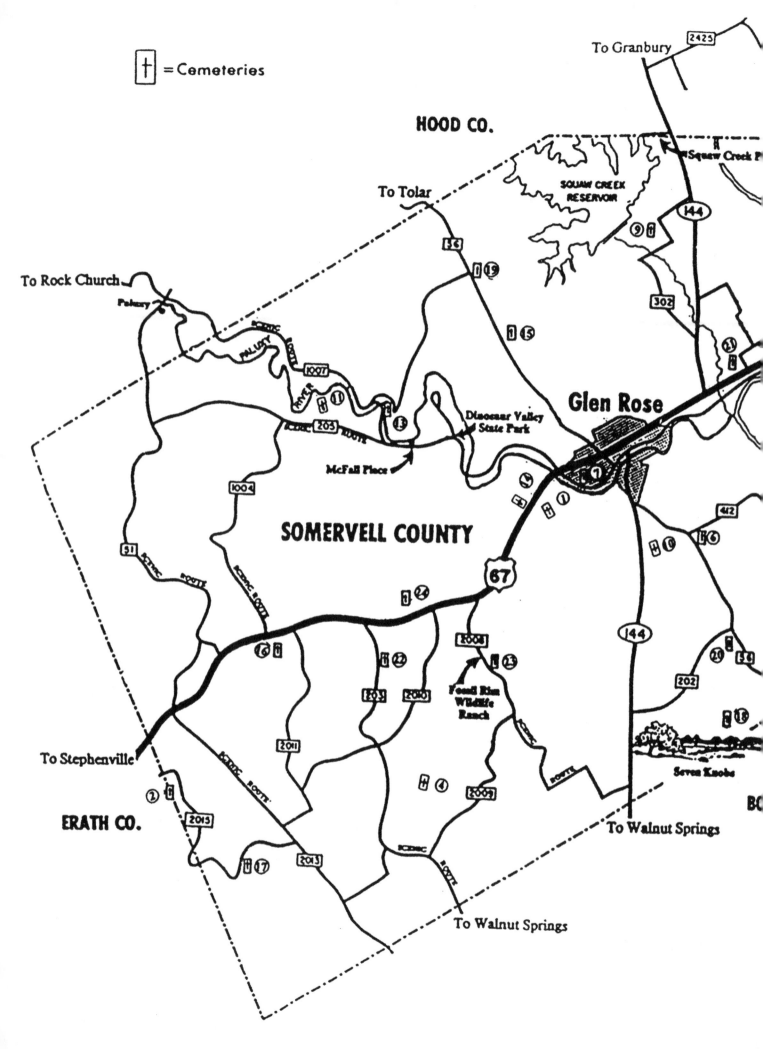

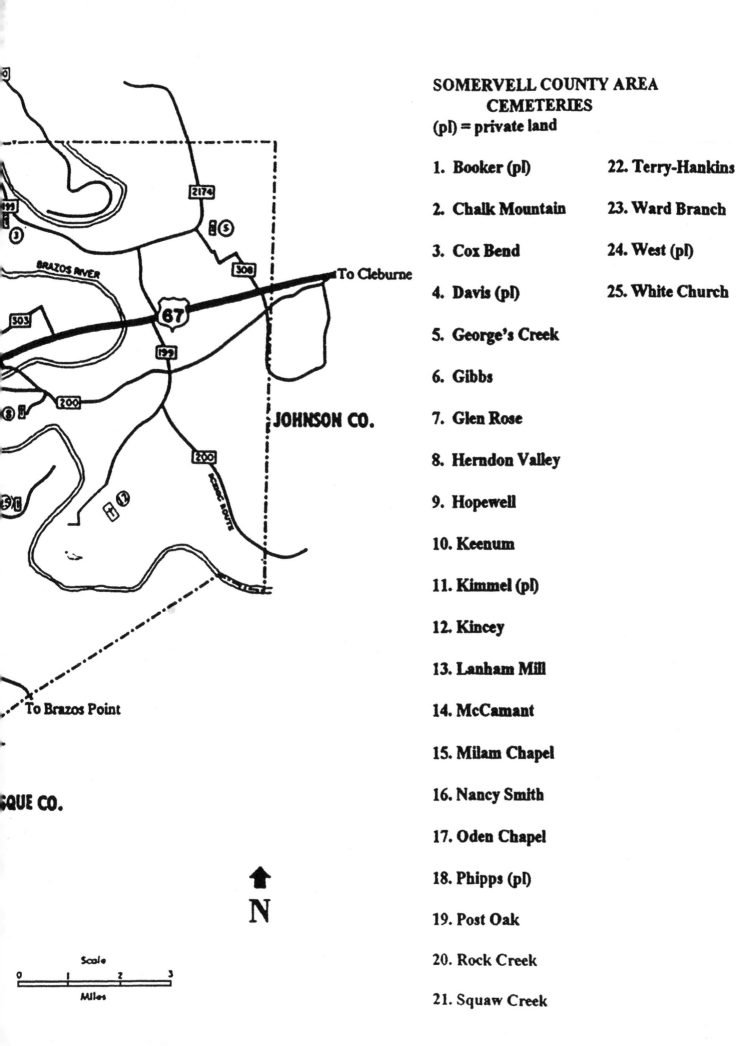

SOMERVELL COUNTY AREA CEMETERIES

(pl) = private land

1. Booker (pl)
2. Chalk Mountain
3. Cox Bend
4. Davis (pl)
5. George's Creek
6. Gibbs
7. Glen Rose
8. Herndon Valley
9. Hopewell
10. Keenum
11. Kimmel (pl)
12. Kincey
13. Lanham Mill
14. McCamant
15. Milam Chapel
16. Nancy Smith
17. Oden Chapel
18. Phipps (pl)
19. Post Oak
20. Rock Creek
21. Squaw Creek
22. Terry-Hankins
23. Ward Branch
24. West (pl)
25. White Church

N

SOMERVELL COUNTY, TEXAS

1896 – 2006

Turner®
Publishing Company

Turner Publishing Company
200 4th Avenue North • Suite 950
Nashville, Tennessee 37219
(615) 255-2665

www.turnerpublishing.com

Library of Congress Control Number: ********

ISBN:978-1-68162-580-5

0 9 8 7 6 5 4 3 2 1

Somervell County Pictoral History

Table of Contents

History

LANHAM MILL COMMUNITY

WILLIAM AND MARY E. LANHAM AND THEIR FAMILY CAME TO TEXAS FROM TENNESSEE ABOUT 1870. THEY PURCHASED LAND AND SETTLED ON A FARM AT THE CONFLUENCE OF THE PALUXY RIVER AND WHITE BLUFF CREEK IN WHAT WAS AT THAT TIME HOOD COUNTY. WILLIAM LANHAM WAS ONE OF 406 CITIZENS WHO SIGNED THE 1875 PETITION TO THE STATE LEGISLATURE THAT LED TO THE CREATION OF SOMERVELL COUNTY OUT OF PORTIONS OF HOOD COUNTY.

BY 1877 LANHAM AND A PARTNER, T. J. HAMICK, OWNED A GRIST MILL LOCATED ON THE PALUXY RIVER ABOUT HALFWAY BETWEEN GLEN ROSE AND PALUXY. THEY BUILT A COTTON GIN ABOUT 1881, AND CONTINUED IN BUSINESS UNTIL A FIRE DESTROYED THE ENTIRE FACILITY IN 1898.

THE AREA AROUND THE MILL OPERATION BECAME KNOWN AS THE LANHAM MILL COMMUNITY. IN ADDITION TO THE MILL AND GIN, THE COMMUNITY INCLUDED FARMS, CHURCHES, A PUBLIC SCHOOL, AND A COMMUNITY CEMETERY. ALTHOUGH LAND FOR THE CEMETERY WAS NOT FORMALLY DEEDED UNTIL 1893, HEADSTONES REVEAL THAT BURIALS OCCURRED HERE AS EARLY AS 1879.

THE COMMUNITY GRADUALLY DECLINED IN THE EARLY 20TH CENTURY, AND BY 1947 THE SCHOOL WAS CLOSED. THE LANHAM MILL CEMETERY REMAINS AS THE LAST PHYSICAL REMNANT OF A ONCE-THRIVING RURAL COMMUNITY.

(1997)

Lanham Mill Community. (Courtesy of Novella Wilson.)

Glen Rose Street Scene. (Courtesy of Becky Ice.)

Pet Parade - 1975. (Courtesy of Sammie Barnard.)

Odd Fellows Lodge picture made by the side of the old George's Creek School Building. (Property of PVA&GS)

Johnetta Crane, Rhonda Duffie, Gizmo - Heritage Center Halloween - 2003.

Group at Lanham Mill. (Courtesy of Novella Wilson.)

*Oak Dale Park, Glen Rose, TX - 1937.
(Property of PVA&GS)*

View of Glen Rose. (Courtesy of J.D. Martin.)

*Whiskey still now located at the Somervell
County Museum. (Courtesy of Novella Wilson.)*

*Hill on left on 67 as you look south toward Glen Rose Ag Bldg.
(Courtesy of Mary Ann Million.)*

*Glen Rose Concert Band. (Courtesy of Theda
Deaver.)*

Texas Bluebonnets. (Courtesy of Connie Scott.)

Town scene. (Courtesy of Connie Scott.)

Downtown Scene. (Courtesy of Connie Scott.)

YWCA Camp. (Courtesy of Connie Scott.)

Ice House. (Courtesy of Connie Scott.)

Glen Lake Camp. (Courtesy of Connie Scott.)

Entrance to Oak Dale. (Courtesy of Connie Scott.)

Community Center, Glen Rose, TX. (Courtesy of Pat Trimble.)

Courthouse, 1891-92.

Original Somervell County Courthouse. (Courtesy of E.B. McCowan.)

Destruction caused by 1902 tornado. Clock faces on the courthouse tower were blown away.

Courthouse

Courthouse - 1925

1986-1990 courthouse renovation. (Courtesy of Becky Ice.)

10

County officials - Somervell County, 1923. Front, l-r: Andrew J. Wilkins, Bob McCallester, _, Mr. Childress, Jim Shackelford; 2nd row: Moss Robinson, _, _, George Booker; back: Walter Davis, George Bess, _, _, John A. Hamberlin. (Courtesy of Kathy Moss.)

Gov. George W. Bush signing HB508 for Somervell County and the city of Glen Rose, Aug. 17, 1999. (Courtesy of Judge Walter Maynard.)

J.P. Griffin, Dist. Judge John Neill, County Treasurer Barbara Hudson, County Judge Walter Maynard, Dist/County Clerk Candy Garrett and Commissioners Barnard and Ramsay. (Courtesy of Judge Walter Maynard.)

Political Rally on the square.

Courthouse. (Courtesy of Connie Scott.)

The beginning city/county partnership to approve courthouse park. (Courtesy of Helen Kerwin.)

Jimmy Gosdin ripping up pavement for park. (Courtesy of Helen Kerwin.)

Larry Hulsey building star on walk next to Star Fountain that his grandfather made. (Courtesy of Helen Kerwin.)

Helen Kerwin and Lila Carter laying out the courthouse park. (Courtesy of Helen Kerwin.)

Courthouse park finished before Christmas. (Courtesy of Helen Kerwin.)

Somervell County Jail. (Courtesy of Pat Trimble.)

Churches

Rainbow Baptist Church baptizing in 1902. John Coats, Pastor. (Courtesy of David Barclay.)

White Church. (Property of PVA&GS)

Post Oak Chapel. (Courtesy of Aaron Judkins.)

First Baptist Church, Glen Rose. (Courtesy of Connie Scott.)

First Methodist Church. (Courtesy of Connie Scott.)

1st row: Judy Osborn, Winnie Merrill, Ada Deason, Ruth Parker, Lizzie Moss, Mary Voss; 2nd row: Mag Miles, Ida Witt, unknown, Maudine Riddle, Irma Firestone, Lottie Hart; 3rd row: Bo Pruitt, Debs Garms. (Courtesy of Billie Flanary.)

Glen Lake Methodist Camp, Glen Rose, TX. (Courtesy of Mary Ann Million.)

Schools

Lanham Mill School House after renovation, Heritage Park. (Courtesy of Helen Kerwin.)

Glen Rose Class of 1954, 1st row: Lindy McFall, Billy (Rives) Flanary, Barbara (Jackson), Maxine (Howard) Chadick, Eddie Flanary; back row: Bonnah (Brawley) Boyd, Kenneth Nabors, Joe Bob Russell, Patti (Daniel) Town, Darwin Marsh, Eldon (Pete) Wilkins, Adel Underwood, Bill Orr, Kenneth Wells, Bertha (Wilson) Mieth, Bill Cooper, Dorothy (Pinson) Gibbs Lewis.

Alta Vista School. Some of those in photo are Fred Morrow, Floyd Morrow, Harrison Hewlett, J.W. Morrow and Jim Hewlett. (Courtesy of Karen Shaw.)

Bugtussel School. (Courtesy of Sammie Barnard.)

Senior Class 1946-47. Back row: Mary Ellen Crouch, Bob Jones, Leon West, W. Russ Rhodes (principal), Roy Lee Mullins, James Hollingsworth, Geneva (Pete) Corley. Bottom row: Erna Jean Daniels, Dora Mae Alexander, Patsy Smith, Mary Ann Pruitt, Mattie Jean Peterson, Charleyne Kelsey, Wanda Swain (Mansfield). Missing from picture: Maxine Noack (O'Neal). (Courtesy of Mattie Jean Jones.)

Mrs. Alsup 6th Grade Class, 1941-42. Top row l-r: Orren, Gary West, Bert Willey, Floyd Parvin, Joe Gordon Whitworth, J.J. Autrey, Bill Osborn, Willard Deason, Carl Beck. 2nd row l-r: Dottie Crabtree, Lila Ratliff, Martha, Leorna Turner, Darlene Smith, Mrs. Alsup, Greer Plummer, Felton Dempsey, Clois Sandlin, Randy Hart. 3rd row l-r: Erna Jean Daniels, Lula Mae Russells, Betty Jo Vaughn, Mary Ann Pruitt, Bonnie Lee Johnson, Jennie Jean Kelly, Betty Plummer, Mary Jo Bohannan, Patsy Smith, Mattie Jean Peterson. Sitting on ground l-r: Windell Rozelle, Kenneth Miller, Billy Jack Sparks, Odell Woodard, Otis, Arthur Newman, James Earl. (Courtesy of Mattie Jean Jones.)

Mrs. Neville Milam's 1st Grade, 1936-37, l-r: Bobby Lee Limbell, W.A., James Earl Baugh, Tammy, J.W. Minns, (on knees) Gordon, Gaylord Dempsey, inside grocery: Martha Barnett, Mattie Jean Peterson, Windell Rozelle, Floyd Parvin, unknown Gosdin. (Courtesy of Mattie Jean Jones.)

Mrs. Lucille Pullen 3rd Grade Class, 1938-39. Top row l-r: Windell Rozelle, Harold Rhodes, Mrs. Pullen, Bruce Frye, Elma Wallace; 2nd row l-r: Bert Willey, Alvin Swanes, Gary West, James Earl Baugh, Odell Woodard, Willard Deason; front row, l-r: _ Barnhill, Mary Ann Pruitt, Betty Jo Vaughn, Dottie Crabtree, Mattie Jean Peterson, Ollie Head, Jessie Lee Henderson, Jennie Jean Kelly, Joy Lee Cocker, _, Bonnie Harber. (Courtesy of Mattie Jean Jones.)

l-r: Murray Walker, James Hollingworth, Bob Jones were seniors in 1946 on football field. (Courtesy of Mattie Jean Jones.)

Eulogy School. (Property of PVA&GS)

Eulogy School. (Property of PVA&GS)

George's Creek, the two story building is George's Creek School. (Property of PVA&GS)

Thorp Spring Christian College Administration Building and students on campus. Picture made sometime after 1910, back in its heyday. (Property of PVA&GS)

Add-Ran University in its last days at Thorp Spring, before moving to Waco. (Property of PVA&GS.)

Pauluxy School - Tommie Howard-teacher. Sitting: Melborn Long, Jake Underwood, Howard Slater, Melvin Slater, Jo Lena Tuck, Fannie Whitaker, Velma McBrear, Buleah Roper, Berton Lernerd, Mr. Howard, Babe Gordon Larnard, Milton Ramfield, Luther Barbee and two little sisters, part of Dick Glen's face behind Luther, Tom Larnard, George Ford, Olie Glen, Harry Wilson, Johnnie Holmes, Doyle Wilson; front: Arthur Holmes with bike, Vonnie Brooks, Harvey McBrear, Tallie Eden, Willie Larnard, Earl Brooks, Bettie Whiteker, Ivy Brooks, Clona Chrits, Winnie Underwood, Zola Slaten, Niecy Ramfield, Nicey Ramfield, Edith Eden, Willie Eiferd, Nola Brooks, _ Crites, Scott Homes, John _, _; 2nd row: Grover Larnard, Johnnie Larnard, John Ford, Howard _, Lillie Etheridge, Bettie Morrison, Walter Larnard, Cora Glen, Burl Lambert, Mollie Slaton, Alice Ford holding her sister Winnie, Mollie Eden, Ethel Eden; on porch: Slaten, Ben Wilson, Henry Holmes, Walter Crites, Phil Baker, Henry Long, Cole Underwood. (Donated by Novella Wilson property of PVA&GS)

Post Oak School. (Courtesy of Nann Martin.)

Play presentation "Old Maid Convention" at Post Oak School around 1900. Cast: Billie Thomas, Annabelle Camp, Mary Bullion, Amanda Camp, Maud Bullion, Jake Newman, Jess Collins, Sarah Jones, Minnie Simons, Elva Denio, Ellen Buzan, Roxie Osborn. (Courtesy of Nann Martin.)

Senior Class 1948-49. Back row: Charles Connally, Don Osborn, Billy Ward, Ted Sulta, Lynn Norman, John Lewis Merrill, Gary Howeth, Logan Starnes, Jimmy Chadick, Donald Ray Flanary. Next row: Louise Wells, Patsy Sparks, Mozelle Moss, Neva Mimms, Jo Corley, Patsy Shackelford, Yvonne Bohannan, Mrs. Terry (teacher), (teacher), Mack Walker. Next row: Virgie Marshall, Catherine Keller, Dorothy Taylor, Glen Eva Sanderson, Billie Keenum, Nellie Helen Mieth, Billie Firestone, Johnnie Faye Carlisle, Betty Lou Harvey; bottom row: Kenneth Burney. (Courtesy of Yvonne Cotton.)

School Basketball Picture, 1946-47. 1st row l-r: Dorothy Taylor, Patsy Sparks, Pete Corley, Erna Jean Daniels, Doris Jones, Eleanor Cheek; 2nd row, Lela Mae McMillin, Catherine Keller, Yvonne Cotton, Coach Williams, Jo Corley, Billie Keenum. (Courtesy of Yvonne Cotton.)

Eulogy School, ca. 1907-08. (Courtesy of Rhonda Duffie.)

21

Hico High School. (Courtesy of Connie Scott.)

Lanham Mill School House before being moved to Heritage Park. (Courtesy of Helen Kerwin.)

3rd grade class at Glen Rose, 1939-40, Patsy's class. (Courtesy of Janie Pulliam and Patsy Odom.)

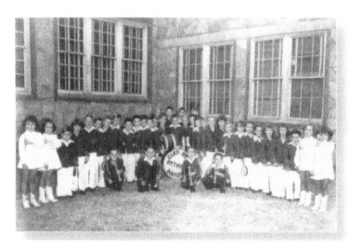

Glen Rose Rhythm Band. (Courtesy of Sammie Barnard.)

Porter School. (Courtesy of David Barclay.)

Herndon Valley or Bug Tussell School. Back row, l-r: Berlin Reeves-teacher, Arvil Bruce, Lois Faulkner, Coll Davis, Clyde Bagby, John Alton "Cotton" Oldham, Simmons Sparks, Dee Sparks, Obie "Tobe" Sparks, Lawrence "Buddy" Bruce, Vertie Sparks, Myrtle Locker. Front: Dora "Dode" Locker, Lillian "Bug" Faulkner, Francis "Frankie" Sawyer, Velma Bruce, Ora Sawyer, Mary Riley and Viva Sawyer. (Courtesy of Maxine Bagby.)

2nd grade, 1937-38, Mrs. Pullen-teacher. (Courtesy of Connie Scott.)

Glen Rose Faculty, 1945-46. (Courtesy of Connie Scott.)

Glen Rose High School, 1944-45 Senior Class; back: Bobby Dotson, Lefty O'Neal, Oscar Archer, George Snyder, Lynn Lane, Jr. Brawley - rest unknown. (Courtesy of Bonnah Boyd.)

Tiger Football Stadium. (Courtesy of Mary Ann Million.)

Glen Rose Elementary School, 1943-44, 2nd grade. (Courtesy of Bonnah Boyd.)

Lower Rock Creek School ca. 1900. Thought to be: back row l-r: Eva Moseley, Pearl Martin, Bill Force, Cora Young-teacher, Tommy Howard, Virgil Reeves, Gus Garner, Range Reeves, Hugh Pruett, Mart Sandlin, Tony Garner and Calvin Wilkins; 2nd row from back: Medelie Wilkerson, George Keenum, Bessie Sandlin, Mattie Plummer, Ina Carriger, Theresa Tissue Garner, Mattie Martin, Myrtle Knight, Sallie Young, Stella Knight, Beulah Young, Buck Wilkins, Elbert Chester; 3rd row: Ira Plummer, Fred Young, Joe Trimble, Zeb Garner, Wayne Hart and Bud Young; front row: William Dennis, Bunch Reeves, Grover Wheatly, Harry Trimble, Wade Dennis, Bill Keenum, Elbert Wilkins, Otis Plummer, Russell Strutton, Lee Young, Clarence Sandlin, Clark Strutton, Carriger boy, Nolan Moseley.

(Courtesy of Ann Daniel.)

Lower Rock Creek School, ca. 1903. (Courtesy of Ann Daniel.)

Lower Rock Creek School ca. 1910. (Courtesy of Ann Daniel.)

Sunday school group at White Church, probably about 1915 or 1916. (Courtesy of Ann Daniel.)

1919 Ft. Spunky School, Ft. Spunky, TX. 1st row: Bill Allen, _, _, Buck Turner, Isom Finley, Tressie Allison, Lorene Allison, Audie Norton, Pauline Pinson, Nova Finely, Daisy Dingler, Ina May Armstrong, _ Orr, Murl Pinson, Harmon Elliott, Lora Finley, Elbert Orr, Vennie Hudgins, Zelma Orr, Kate Barnard; 2nd row: Mr. Curl-teacher, Garland Howeth, Wallace Pinson, Earl Elliott, Raymond Styron, Arlie Cheek, Clark Cavasos, Orville Pinson, David Myers. (Courtesy of Susan Boy.)

Business

First National Bank of Glen Rose. (Property of PVA&GS)

View of Barnard's Mill when it was a hospital.

Barnard's Mill. (Courtesy of Sammie Barnard and James Barnard.)

Texaco Station. (Courtesy of Becky Ice.)

Paul Hatler. (Courtesy of Rhonda Duffie.)

Company owned by Paul Hatler. (Courtesy of Rhonda Duffie.)

Francis Rives in front of Rives Café. (Courtesy of Billie Flanary.)

Hopewell Post Office. (Courtesy of Aaron Judkins.)

Post Office, Glass, TX. (Courtesy of Rhonda Duffie.)

Bank building

Old bank building - July 1949. (Loyd Don Moss Collection.)

Comanche Peak Power Station. (Courtesy of Betty Gosdin.)

Palace Theater 1942. (Courtesy of Mattie Jean Jones.)

Joe Russell Sr. with wife May with delivery truck in front of Glen Rose famous mineral water. (Courtesy of Russ Miller.)

Joe Russell Sr. with Glen Rose famous mineral water bottle at well. (Courtesy of Russ Miller.)

Glen Rose Hotel lobby - 1956. (Courtesy of Russ Miller.)

Glen Rose Hotel postcard - 1929. (Courtesy of Russ Miller.)

Glen Rose Hotel return address on envelope. (Courtesy of Russ Miller.)

Russell's Café in Grand Prairie during WWII. (Courtesy of Russ Miller.)

Chalk Mountain

Oakdale Park Art Gallery, 1967; l-r: W.B. Cowan, Bob Summers, Judge Temple Summers, Willie Flippin, Seraphie Riddle, Rosemary Rheinlander, Novella Wilson, Anne Moss, Eva Howeth, Loree Norman, Theresa Wallace, Lola Bowers, Fayrene McPherson, Adele Cowan, Chloe Buzan.

Watermelon Party. Left side: Nona Lawrence, Betty Gosdin, Marguerite Dempsey, Jackie Terry, Margie Price, Helen Young and Wendie Trimble. (Courtesy of Novella Wilson.)

John and Novella (May) Wilson. (Courtesy of Novella Wilson.)

Loma Swaim, Novella's first art teacher. (Courtesy of Novella Wilson.)

Wendy Trimble. (Courtesy of Novella Wilson.)

Novella's Art Gallery, Walker Street, Glen Rose, TX. (Courtesy of Novella Wilson.)

Vivian and Don Hill Variety and Hardware Store. (Property of PVA&GS)

Roden Drug Store. (Donated by Bonnah Boyd, property of PVA&GS)

Jim Lilly in store. (Property of PVA&GS)

Tom's Hamburgers. (Courtesy of Paul Bone.)

The Corner Drug Store located on Barnard Street; presently TXU Building. (Property of PVA&GS)

Dick Williams Station.

Lilly Store. (Goldsmith Collection, property of PVA&GS)

Wilson Brothers Gas Station. (Property of PVA&GS)

Talley Building. (Property of PVA&GS)

The Talley Buidling located on the square. (Property of PVA&GS)

The Wemp Hotel. (Property of PVA&GS)

Rudy Lane Station. (Property of PVA&GS)

Shields & Son Furniture, Hardware and Undertakers. (Courtesy of Rhonda Duffie.)

T.C. Passenger Station. Hico, Texas. (Courtesy of Connie Scott.)

First National Bank. (Courtesy of PVA&GS)

River Crest.

Casino at Oak Dale Park. (Courtesy of Connie Scott.)

Picture taken inside Lane Ford Motor Co. On left is John B. Wilson. (Courtesy of Janie Pulliam and Patsy Odom.)

Telephone building being moved to Heritage Park. (Courtesy of Helen Kerwin.)

Telephone building after it was renovated. (Courtesy of Helen Kerwin.)

M.L. Bunt and his Watkins Wagon in the street at Rainbow in the fall of 1907. The Watkins peddler was a familiar sight around the local communities. (Courtesy of David Barclay.)

A bunch of boys whooping it up in front of the Rainbow Barber Shop. (Courtesy of David Barclay.)

Uncle of Little Joe Bunt. (Courtesy of David Barclay.)

Official Marker on Campbell Building. (Property of PVAGS.)

Lane & Sons Motor Co., Glen Rose, TX. (Courtesy of Mary Ann Million.)

The Campbell Building.

Campbell Stable.

Medical

Jameson Nurs-o-tel. (Courtesy of Brenda Ransom.)

Dr. Johnson's Sanitarium, Glen Rose, TX. (Courtesy of Becky Ice.)

Gaither Sanitarium. (Donated by Novella Wilson, property of PVA&GS)

Across the street from Snyder Sanitariam. Was between Hereford and Cedar Sts. on Barnard St.

Milling Sanitarium, petrified wood home. (Courtesy of Adele Cowan, property of PVA&GS)

Pilgrams Sanitarium. (Property of SCGHS.)

Snyder's Sanitarium. (Courtesy of Connie Scott.)

37

Judy, the ostrich

Fern Newman Cornelius and Judy the Ostrich, Oct. 30, 1926. (Courtesy of Bonnah Boyd.)

Dr. Snyder's Drugless Sanitarium, Glen Rose, TX. (Courtesy of Novella Wilson.)

(Property of PVA&GS)

Hanna Hospital

Homes

The Glass homeplace ca. 1910, Somervell County. William Glass, Mary Jane (Lafon) Glass and daughters l-r: Florence Glass McFaddin, Addie Glass Ervin, Vena Glass Walton McFadin, Sharon Glass Echols. (Courtesy of Joan Taylor.)

The home of Silas Scott Offutt - County Line Road, Somervell County, TX. (Courtesy of Peggy Huffman.)

C.A. Bridges, Ona Bridges - Bridges home overlooking Barnard St. (Courtesy of Mary Lee Bridges.)

May family home. (Courtesy of Novella Wilson.)

George P. Snyder Residence, Glen Rose, TX. (Courtesy of Becky Ice. and Connie Scott.)

Pancake Ranch 4-1/2 miles SW of Cranfills Gap, TX. (Courtesy of Becky Ice.)

John St. Helen Cabin. (Courtesy of Aaron Judkins.)

Eula and Beulah Jones at their home. (Courtesy of Luther Kelly.)

Eula and Beulah Jones at their home. (Courtesy of Luther Kelly.)

Dr. Gus A. Snyder home. (Courtesy of Connie Scott.)

41

Campbell House. (Courtesy of Connie Scott.)

House on corner of Vernon and Vine (now a city parking lot) was once owned by Mr. Matney who was a cobbler in one of the shops in bottom of Talley Bldg., 1948. (Courtesy of Pat Trimble.)

In front of the old homeplace in Potts Valley between Glen Rose and Walnut Springs, TX. Grandpa Pace with two of his nieces on the porch, Aunt Matt Clayton and her son J.T., daughters Virgie, Lesha and Bertha. The house is still standing. (Courtesy of Clodell Davis.)

Proctor and Alice (Row) Mann's home at Potts Valley. (Courtesy of Irene (Mann) Jolly.)

Roads & Transportation

Lafette King - Brazos River Bridge. (Courtesy of Nann Martin.)

Hwy 67 Bridge. (Courtesy of Sammie Barnard.)

Main Street looking north, Glen Rose, TX, postcard. (Courtesy of Russ Miller.)

Low Water Bridge dedication. (Property of PVA&GS)

Farmer Who Filed Suit To Stop Traffic Sells Out

GLEN ROSE, Nov. 22 (Spl) — Ed Edwards, farmer in the Cox's Bend community of Somervell County, who was placed under a $1,000 peace bond Tuesday because of alleged efforts to close a road through his property, has sold out.

It was announced Saturday that J. M. Russell, hotel proprietor and landowner and former mayor here, has purchased the 200-acre tract Edwards bought several months ago.

Soon after acquiring the land, Edwards filed a civil suit against county officials, seeking a restraining order to prevent traffic through his property. The restraining order was denied.

Last Sunday, witnesses testified at a hearing before Judge Penn Jackson in 18th District Court here Tuesday, a sign went up on a tree beside the road. It read:

"No trespassing. This road is private property and will be mined with high explosives."

In the absence of County Attorney E. T. Adams, District Attorney John A. James of Cleburne

County Court, alleging that the farmer had threatened human life, and applied in district court for a peace bond.

Edwards testified that he had planned only to discharge dynamite on his land to loosen the earth around fruit trees near the road. State witnesses said the road had been used as a public thoroughfare for 50 years.

Cooke Centennial Plans Started

GAINESVILLE, Nov. 22 (Spl). A committee composed of Roy P. Wilson and A. Morton Smith of the Cooke County Fair Board has been named to invite each of 50 or more civic, fraternal and social clubs in Gainesville and Cooke County to name representatives on a Cooke County centennial commission to plan a month-by-month celebration.

Cooke County was created March 20, 1848. The commission will meet here again in January to

Joe Russell Sr. buys acreage to stop dispute. (Courtesy of Russ Miller.)

Near Glen View Park, Glen Rose, TX. (Property of PVA&GS)

Brazos Point Bridge dedication. (Courtesy of Rhonda Duffie.)

"Among the Cedars" near Chalk Mountain, TX. (Courtesy of Rhonda Duffie.)

Blue Hole Crossing. (Courtesy of Novella Wilson.)

"The Dip" Hwy. 205. (Courtesy of Mary Ann Million.)

The dedication of the first bridge across the Brazos between Granbury and Waco. Prior to the construction of the bridge only a ferry was available; consequently most trade was through Granbury because the crossing to Cleburne was too uncertain. (Courtesy of David Barclay.)

Downtown Bridge. (Courtesy of Connie Scott.)

Auto Park. (Courtesy of Connie Scott.)

Main Street, Hico, TX. (Courtesy of Connie Scott.)

Hico, TX. (Courtesy of Connie Scott.)

Santa Fe Railroad, Cleburne, TX. (Courtesy of Rhonda Duffie.)

The Motorway, Glen Rose, TX in front of the Campbell Building.

Waterways

Lakeview Park. (Courtesy of Pat Trimble.)

Brazos River at Low Water Bridge - May 1957. Luther Million wearing hat. (Courtesy of Dorthy Ketter.)

Glen Rose flood. (Courtesy of Becky Ice.)

Brazos River flood at the Low Water Bridge, Somervell County. (Courtesy of Becky Ice.)

Joe Russell Jr. on Paluxy Dam behind Glen Rose Hotel. (Courtesy of Russ Miller.)

Oakdale Park. (Courtesy of Pete May.)

Bathing pool on Plauxy River, Glen Rose, TX. (Courtesy of Vivian and Don Hill.)

Lake at Lakeview Park, Glen Rose, TX. (Property of PVA&GS)

The Morton Well. (Courtesy of Connie Scott.)

Lover's Leap, Lakeview Park, Glen Rose, TX. (Property of PVA&GS)

Lake View Park. (Courtesy of Connie Scott.)

Paluxy River Dam. (Courtesy of Connie Scott.)

Lake View Park. (Courtesy of Connie Scott.)

Churn Well. (Courtesy of Connie Scott.)

3" Flowing Well. (Courtesy of Connie Scott.)

Lake View Park. (Courtesy of Connie Scott.)

Oak Dale Park. (Courtesy of Connie Scott.)

Stump Well, Lake View Park. (Courtesy of Connie Scott.)

Paluxy River. (Courtesy of Connie Scott.)

Paluxy River. (Courtesy of Connie Scott.)

Sulphur Falls, Glen Rose, TX. (Courtesy of Connie Scott.)

51

Dinosaurs

Tannon Judkins at Dinosaur Valley tracks. (Courtesy of Aaron Judkins.)

A sign built onto the bandstand intended to help show visitors to the "Valley of the Dinosaurs." (Property of PVA&GS)

Dinosaur Tracks, Mr. Ryals. (Donated by Novella Wilson.)

Dinosaur track excavation at Dinosaur Valley State Park, Glen Rose, TX. (Courtesy of Novella Wilson.)

Turnage Patton trail. (Courtesy of Aaron Judkins.)

Tannon Judkins in dino track. (Courtesy of Aaron Judkins.)

Dinosaur Track excavation at Dinosaur Valley State Park, Glen Rose, TX. (Courtesy of Novella Wilson.)

Ernest Tolbert "Bull" Adams cataloguing dinosaur bones. (Courtesy of Mary Adams.)

(Courtesy of Roland T. Bird.)

People watching excavation of dinosaur tracks. (Courtesy of Roland T. Bird.)

Dinosaur track excavation. . (Courtesy
of Roland T. Bird.)

Dinosaur track excavation. . (Courtesy of
Roland T. Bird.)

Roland T. Bird.

Roland T. Bird.

Roland T. Bird.

Families

John J. and Sarh "Sallie" (Gosdin) James and children: William L. (b. 1894), Lucy Ann (b. 1896), Fannie Frances (b. 1898) and Buck. (Courtesy of Betty J. Gosdin.)

Tressi Allison Styron, Burl Barnard, James Edward Barnard, Marlie Edward Barnard, Marie Kelly Barnard, William "Bill" Morrison. (Courtesy of Sammie Barnard)

Billy and Robena Miller family - 1968, l-r: Jack Miller, Bob Miller, Bill Miller, Nancy Miller Moore, Connie Miller Scott. (Courtesy of Connie Scott.)

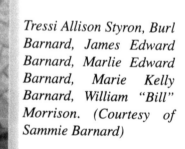

Jess and Vida (Suratt) Parvin. (Courtesy of Yvonne Cotton.)

l-r: Carol Bohannan, Yvonne Bohannan, Grace Bohannan, Conroe Bohannan. (Courtesy of Yvonne Cotton.)

James Donald Cotton and Yvonne Bohannan Cotton. (Courtesy of Yvonne Cotton.)

Back row: Billy Blackwell, Emma Jane Blackwell Boggs, John Blackwell, Mamie Blackwell Sawyer; front: Francis Marion Blackwell, Rebecca Caroline (Hayes) Blackwell. (Courtesy of Yvonne Cotton.)

Grandmother Knight's birthday party. Jack Buzan, Florence Knight, Myrtle Buzan, Rosemary Bell, Joel Buzan and Rosemary's mother Mary E. Bell at the home of Ruby and Dawson Holden on S.W. Barnard St., Glen Rose, TX. (Courtesy of Mary Elizabeth Bell.)

Front: Harrison Boggs and Emma Blackwell Boggs; back: Beulah Boggs O'Neal, Grace Boggs Bohannon, Martha Boggs Scifres. (Courtesy of Yvonne Cotton.)

Grandmother Sina Ann Buzan, Joel, Jack and Douglas at her home (old homestead, Glen Rose). (Courtesy of Mary Elizabeth Bell.)

l-r: George Hamberlin, Harry Hamberlin, Dora Hamberlin Moss, Florence E. Knight. Standing behind Florence is Lallah H. Moss at old home place on Paluxy. (Courtesy of Mary Elizabeth Bell.)

Christmas 1962 at Myrtle Buzan's home just after Joe Buzan's death which occurred Sept. 15, 1962; l-r: Myrtle Buzan, Brenda Buzan, Mary E. Bell (behind Brenda), Dan Buzan, Bill Buzan, Jack Buzan, Douglas Buzan, Harold J. Buzan, Joel Buzan and Rosemary Bell. (Courtesy of Mary Elizabeth Bell.)

August 1961 at the home of Joe and Myrtle Buzan; 1st row l-r: David Cave, James Cave, Brenda Buzan; 2nd row: Mary Elizabeth (Buzan) Bell, Myrtle and Joe Buzan, Annie Buzan, Almarine Merril, Erlene Cave and Rosemary. (Courtesy of Mary Elizabeth Bell.)

Mary Elizabeth and Harry Bell, Centennial June 7, 1975, Glen Rose, TX. (Courtesy of Mary Elizabeth Bell.)

l-r: Dan, Myrtle, Joseph E. and Harold J. Buzan. Taken at Harry and Mary Elizabeth Bell's home in Glen Rose, TX, Spring Town. (Courtesy of Mary Elizabeth Bell.)

Wm. "Bill" Luther Knight and baby daughter Billie Frances Knight. Bill Knight was only son of Reuben Messenger Knight Jr. and Florence Eller Knight. (Courtesy of Mary Elizabeth Bell.)

l-r: Dan Buzan, Mary Elizabeth (Buzan) Bell, Joe Buzan and Harold J. Buzan out in front of Harry and Mary Elizabeth Bell's house in Spring Town section of Glen Rose, TX. (Courtesy of Mary Elizabeth Bell.)

Florence Knight and her daughters: Ruby, Annie, Myrtle and twins, Estella and Adella. (Courtesy of Mary Elizabeth Bell.)

Jacob Richard Buzan, Sina Ann (Simpson) Buzan. (Courtesy of Mary Elizabeth Bell.)

Ruby Knight, Myrtle B. Buzan, Mary Elizabeth (Buzan) Bell. (Courtesy of Mary Elizabeth Bell.)

Reuben M. Knight and wife Florence E. (Hamberlin) Knight, son William, Bell's daughter Johnnie Ruby and Annie Knight. (Courtesy of Mary Elizabeth Bell.)

Mary E. Buzan Bell, Rosemary Bell Jobe, James Harry Bell, Amanda Jobe, Melanie Jobe Piekarsky.

l-r: Barbara Isabella (Buzan) Fox; Annie Mae Keeters, Nancy E. (Buzan) Cromwell, Jacob Richard Buzan, Mary J. (Buzan) Earley, Zora (Cromwell) Keeters Fulfer, Sina Ann (Simpson) Buzan (wife of Jacob Richard Buzan), Frank Fulfer (Zora's husband). (Courtesy of Mary Elizabeth Bell.)

Joseph E. Buzan, Myrtle B. Knight Buzan, 1957. (Courtesy of Mary Elizabeth Bell.)

Kenneth Ray "Ken" Gilleland, Helene Waltraud Gotz Bishop Gilleland, Wendy Marie Gilleland. (Courtesy of Betty J. Gosdin.)

Standing l-r: Raina Lynn and Cara Sue Gilleland; middle: Paula Diane (Marrs) and Michael Lynn Gilleland; bottom: Samantha Gilleland. (Courtesy of Betty J. Gosdin.)

l-r: David and Stacy Jones, Sharon and Bob Gilleland, Melissa and Greg Gilleland and baby Abby Gilleland. (Courtesy of Betty J. Gosdin.)

Charles Wayne and Sharon Rena (Williams) Gilleland, Eric Wade and Beth Colleen. (Courtesy of Betty J. Gosdin.)

61

Lorene (Gosdin) Gilleland and Andrew Jesse "Jack" Gilleland. (Courtesy of Betty J. Gosdin.)

Back l-r: James Dorson "Jim," J.B., Delia Rose (Offutt), Willie Lucille; front: Theodore Jackson "Red" Gosdin. (Courtesy of Betty J. Gosdin.)

Back l-r: William Arvil "Willie" Shipman, William "Chad" Shipman, Stephanie Nicole Shipman; front: Judy Darlene (Gosdin) Shipman - May 1989. (Courtesy of Betty J. Gosdin.)

Back l-r: Pamela Kaye (Huffman) Parsons, Kimberly (Huffman) Gass; front: Joe Huffman and Peggy (Odom) Huffman. (Courtesy of Peggy Huffman.)

Terri Lynn Sturgeon, daughter of Carol Gartrell. (Courtesy of Janelle Gartrell.)

John Sturgeon and Carol Gartrell. (Courtesy of Janelle Gartrell.)

Michael Brimer and Mitchell Brimer. (Courtesy of Janelle Gartrell.)

l-r: Carol (Gartrell) Shadell holding Danny Shadell and Raymond Shadell holding Teresa Shadell. (Courtesy of Janelle Gartrell.)

l-r: Teresa Shadell, Raymond Shadell, Danny Shadell. (Courtesy of Janelle Gartrell.)

Moody Booker.

Annie E. Boyd, Nellie B. Boyd. (Courtesy of Rhonda Duffie.)

George W. Boyd, Napoleon B. Boyd, William R. Boyd. (Courtesy of Rhonda Duffie.)

Launching Lone Star March 25, 1915; l-r: Myrtle, Marfie, Maud, Hiram, Don Thomas. (Courtesy of Sammie Barnard and James Barnard.)

l-r: Jed Bridges, Jessica Bridges (standing), Jaci Bridges, Jaylan Evans, Jace Bridges, Mama Lou. (Courtesy of J. Weldon Bridges.)

l-r: Mary Lee Bridges, Jack Bridges Jr. (Courtesy of J. Weldon Bridges.)

l-r: Jill Bridges, Jim Bob Bridges, J. Weldon Bridges, Jennifer Bridges. (Courtesy of J. Weldon Bridges.)

July 1988, l-r: Jack Weldon Bridges IV, Jack Weldon Bridges III, Jack Weldon Bridges Sr., Jack Weldon Bridges Jr. (Courtesy of J. Weldon Bridges.)

C.A. Bridges, Ona Bridges. (Courtesy of J. Weldon Bridges.)

l-r: Bobbie Lou Bridges, Jack Bridges Jr. (Courtesy of J. Weldon Bridges.)

65

Barnard home, Waco, TX. Mary Ross Barnard in foreground. (Texas Collection, Baylor University - Courtesy of Betty J. Gosdin.)

Marlie Edward Barnard, Marie Olga (Kelly) Barnard. (Courtesy of Sammie Barnard.)

Myrtle (Barnard) Richie and Hugh Richie. Myrtle is daughter of John B. and Narcissus (Nall) Barnard. (Courtesy of Sammie Barnard.)

Ken Barnard and Stacy Lanette (Lane) Barnard, Samuel Lane, Lauren Nichole Barnard. (Courtesy of Sammie Barnard.)

Sammie (Oldham) Barnard, James Edward Barnard. (Courtesy of Sammie Barnard.)

Carrie (Barnard) Chism, Ty Chism, Fisher Chism. (Courtesy of Sammie Barnard.)

Larry, Jennifer, Justin and Jared Roberts - 1996. (Courtesy of Jennifer Roberts.)

Justin Wyman Roberts, age 5; Jared Curtis Roberts, age 3. (Courtesy of Jennifer Roberts.)

"Big" Jack Bridges. (Courtesy of Jennifer Roberts.)

Luckstead family, back l-r: Kay and Eric Luckstead, Rusty and Stephanie Luckstead, Brad and Ann (Luckstead) Gosdin; front: Margie, Sarah, Mattea, Luke and Gene Luckstead. (Courtesy of Betty J. Gosdin.)

Williams Family. (Courtesy of Mary Lee Bridges.)

Larry and Nancy Wilson family. (Courtesy of Mary Lee Bridges.)

Jack Buzan, Irene Martin Buzan, Douglas Buzan and Joel Buzan. (Courtesy of J.D. Martin.)

John Anthony Hamberlin's 80th birthday Sept. 1, 1926 at homestead on Paluxy River Somervell County, Glen Rose, TX. 1st row front: Johnny Rachel Underwood, Jack Buzan, Lloyd Don Moss and George Hamberlin; 2nd row: Dorothy and Walterin Davis, Florence Knight holding Billie Frances Knight, Susan Hamberlin, John A. Hamberlin and Emma Smith. 3rd row: W.B. Dan Buzan, Roy Garner, Mary Elizabeth Buzan and Oliver Fay Trimble; 4th row: Reubin M. Knight, Hattie Moss, Frances Knight, Charlie Moss, Fay Moss Trimble, Maude Moss Barclay and friend, and Annie Knight; 5th row: directly behind Reubin Knight is Earl Mosley, Grandy Moss, William Bill Knight, Joe Buzan, Myrtle Buzan, Ruby Knight, Lester Trimble and behind him is Lalla Moss and unknown man. The last two women are Joana Hamberlin and Adella Davis holding baby Bitty Davis. (Courtesy of Mary Elizabeth Bell.)

John Anthony Hamberlin, Suzan Givens Hamberlin homeplace 1st crossing Paluxy River. (Courtesy of Mary Elizabeth Bell.)

Howard E. Brawley Jr., Howard E. Brawley Sr., Lauree Brawley, Bonnah Faye Brawley, ca. 1946. (Courtesy of Bonnah Fay Brawley.)

Onnie C. Haney Brawley Hudson. (Courtesy of Bonnah Fay Brawley.)

Knight family, l-r: William Luther Knight, Reuben Knight, Ruby Holden, Florence Knight, Anne Knight. (Courtesy of Mrs. Roger English.)

Moss family, back row: John Moss, Red Moss, Bun Moss, Rusty Moss, Thomas Moss, Hossy Moss, Lois Moss, Verna Moss, Sue Moss, Dora Moss, Bea Moss, Thelma Moss, Helen Moss. (Courtesy of Mrs. Roger English.)

Top row l-r: Ben Nabors, Virgil Nabors, Kay Nabors, J.B. (Wheeler) Nabors; seated: Pearl (Nabors) Daniel, Sadie (Nabors) Norman, Minnie Norman, Buster Nabors, Grace (Nabors) McCarthy. (Courtesy of Verna (Daniels) Mills.)

Andrew Grass and family, Rosebud, TX, 1892. (Photo Courtesy of Joan Taylor)

Front: Vera Tidwell Barnes, Laura Ogden, Stephanie Barnes Ogden and James Barnes; back: Tim Ogden Jr., Stephen Ogden and Tim Ogden. (Courtesy of Vera Barnes.)

Rube Chitwood and family.

Wade, Melissa, Spencer and Lynlee Bush. (Courtesy of Peggy Bush.)

Jewel Tidwell Merritt and husband, Hubert Merritt. Jewel is daughter of Aaron and Reta Tidwell. (Courtesy of Vera Barnes.)

Julie Day, Delaine (Bush) Day, Justin Day. (Courtesy of Peggy Bush.)

71

Todd, Andrea, Cameron, Taryn Bush. (Courtesy of Peggy Bush.)

Curtis Bush, Peggy Bush. (Courtesy of Peggy Bush.)

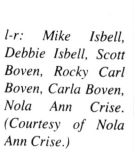

l-r: Mike Isbell, Debbie Isbell, Scott Boven, Rocky Carl Boven, Carla Boven, Nola Ann Crise. (Courtesy of Nola Ann Crise.)

1404 George Thomas Beasley, Catherine (Colledge) Beasley. (Courtesy of Johnny Martin.)

l-r: Lizzie Elizabeth Aston, Ivy Mae Hulsey, Nora Bell Miller, Mary Jane May, Henry Walter Beasley. (Courtesy of Johnny Martin.)

Doris and John D. Fenn - Labor Day 1992. (Courtesy of Pat Trimble.)

l-r: Isabelle McCoy, Billye Jean Trimble, John Calvin McCoy. (Courtesy of Pat Trimble.)

Twins, Virgil and Virgie McCoy. (Courtesy of Pat Trimble.)

Virgil McCoy, son J.R. and Isabelle McCoy holding baby Jim. (Courtesy of Pat Trimble.)

Cecil Ted Fretwell, son of Scott and Lovie Fretwell - 1930. (Courtesy of Pat Trimble.)

Walter B. Syor and Mary Etta (Wood) Syor family. (Courtesy of Wanda Mason.)

McPherson family five generations. Back: Billy Loyd McPherson, Ester, Michelle Moore, Shelly Moore, Billy Gay. (Courtesy of Carol Winters.)

McCarty reunion held at Oak Dale Park. Bryant McCarty with sisters Bertha, Dora, Pauline and Tennie. (Courtesy of Wanda Mason.)

Wanda (McCarty) Sanderson, Alden Lonnie Sanderson. (Courtesy of Wanda Mason.)

William Hamilton McCarty, Mary Ellen (Parker) McCarty. (Courtesy of Wanda Mason.)

McFarlin family. Back: Wayne; middle: Hubert, Patricia, Juanita; front: Michael

Lewis Lee Mears, Wanda Ruth (Taylor) Mears. (Courtesy of Rhonda Duffie.)

Dennis Moore, Charles Moore and Melanie Moore. (Courtesy of Mary Ann Million.)

Bottom row: Melvin Moore, Della (Mann) Moore; back row: Louise (Moore) Gartrell, Mary Ann (Moore) Million, Charles Moore. (Courtesy of Mary Ann Million.)

Early Anderson Moseley. (Courtesy of Kathy Moss.)

Mary Ophelia (Long) Moseley. (Courtesy of Kathy Moss.)

75

Back l-r: Bessie Morrow Beard, Lora Morrow Duncan, Ina Mae Morrow Cooke; front: Floyd Morrow, J.W. Morrow, Ina Hewlett Morrow, Fred Morrow. (Courtesy of Betty Marie Beard.)

Mary Ophelia (Long) Moseley, Helen Loree (Moseley) Newkirk, Ula (Moseley) Sandlin and Andrew (cat); standing: Grace Moseley.

Hugh Morrow Family; Standing: Harold. Seated: Eva, Linda, Kenneth, Donald, Hugh Morrow (Courtesy of Mary Morrow Jones.)

Christmas 2002. Wayne, Linda, Pattie, Jennie Morrow. (Courtesy of Mary Morrow Jones.)

Capt. John W. Morrow, Mary (Hague) Morrow. (Courtesy of Betty Marie Beard.)

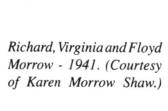

Richard, Virginia and Floyd Morrow - 1941. (Courtesy of Karen Morrow Shaw.)

76

Daisy Viola (Ryals) and George Alvis May. (Courtesy of Novella Wilson.)

Wedding picture in 1899 of John Wesley Morrow and Ina Lee (Hewlett) Morrow. (Courtesy of Mary Morrow Jones.)

June Ray (Wood) and Marvin Lee May. (Courtesy of Novella Wilson.)

Genevia Jane (Corley) and Thomas Alton May. (Courtesy of Novella Wilson.)

Vivian Euclit May, Dora Annie May. (Courtesy of Novella Wilson.)

John D. Wilson and Jessie Novella (May) Wilson. (Courtesy of Novella Wilson.)

l-r: Isaac Newton May, Lela Camila May (in back), Elizabeth Florida "Dollie" (Williams) May holding baby, Vivian Euclit May. (Courtesy of Novella Wilson.)

l-r: Truman Beard, Floyd Morrow, Bessie Morrow Beard with Betty Marie Beard, Ina Mae Morrow, Fred Morrow, Wesley Morrow, Ina Lee Hewlett Morrow, Vernon Pinson holding son Kenneth Pinson. (Courtesy of Mary Morrow Jones.)

Back l-r: Jan Morrow, Wendell Morrow, Sherri Morrow, Gayle Morrow, Jonathan Morrow, Herb Smith, David Morrow; middle row: Chris Jackson, Mara Jackson, Ann Smith, Louise Morrow, Marie Morrow; front row: Jennifer Jackson, Joshua Jackson, Mildred Morrow, Fred Morrow, Quinton Anderson, Angela Anderson, Renee Morrow. (Courtesy of Mr. and Mrs. Fred Morrow.)

1966, l-r: Ann Morrow, Cathy Morrow, Sylvia Morrow, Karen Morrow, Dinah Dement. (Courtesy of Mary Morrow Jones.)

Back l-r: Bessie Morrow Beard and Truman Beard with their children l-r: Betty Marie, Wesley, Lillie Pearl Harris (Higginbottom). (Courtesy of Mary Morrow Jones.)

John Thomas Hewlett family. Back l-r: Olin P. Hewlett, Fannie MacMahon, Alfred Hewlett, Floyd Hewlett, Clarence Hewlett, Sara E. Cheek. (Courtesy of Carolyn M. Kuklies.)

Back l-r: Carolyn Cooke Kuklies, Milton Kuklies; children l-r: Steven Kuklies, Melissa Kuklies. (Courtesy of Mary Morrow

Roy and Lora Morrow Duncan and sons, Wendell and Hewlett. (Courtesy of Carolyn M. Kuklies.)

John Thomas Hewlett, Frances Eugenia Walker Hewlett. (Courtesy of Carolyn M. Kuklies.)

Back l-r: Bessie Morrow, Ina Mae Morrow, Pearl Morrow; front l-r: Lora Morrow, Ina Lee Hewlett Morrow.

John Wayne Morrow. (Courtesy of Mary Morrow Jones.)

Brenda Stewart Maynard, Amy Lynn Maynard, Mattie Armstrong Stewart. (Courtesy of Walter Maynard.)

Ken Maynard. (Courtesy of Walter Maynard.)

Brendon Taylor, son of David Taylor and Tracy Million. (Courtesy of Mary Ann Million.)

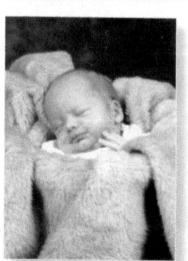

Jacob David Taylor, son of John David Taylor and Tracy Million Taylor. (Courtesy of Mary Ann Million.)

Nathan Cole Sanders, son of Mike Sanders and Angela Million. (Courtesy of Mary Ann Million.)

Brian Sanders, son of Mike Sanders and Angela Million. (Courtesy of Mary Ann Million.)

Michael "Kevin" Sanders, son of Michael Sanders and Angela Million. (Courtesy of Mary Ann Million.)

Tracy Million Taylor. (Courtesy of Mary Ann Million.)

Jennifer Sanders, daughter of Michael Sanders and Angela Million. (Courtesy of Mary Ann Million.)

Angela Danielle (Million) Sanders, daughter of Glennis Million and Mary Ann Million. (Courtesy of Mary Ann Million.)

Ada (Million) Shackelford and husband Hal Shackelford. Ada is daughter of P.W. Million and Texanna Lee. (Courtesy of Mary Ann Million.)

Jerry E. Click and wife Jewell Million, daughter of P.W. Million and Texanna Lee. (Courtesy of Mary Ann Million.)

Minnie Jewel Million, daughter of P.W. Million and Texanna Lee. (Courtesy of Mary Ann Million.)

Sylvia Million, daughter of P.W. Million and Texanna Lee. (Courtesy of Mary Ann Million.)

Sitting: Glennis Million, Alvis Million, Dorthy (Million) Ketter; standing: Mary Ann (Moore) Million, Paul S. Ketter. (Courtesy of Mary Ann Million.)

Paula Jean Ketter, daughter of Dorothy Million and Paul Ketter. (Courtesy of Mary Ann Million.)

Jerry Click and wife Jewel (Million) Click. (Courtesy of Mary Ann Million.)

Billie (Shackelford) Bridges and husband Roy Bridges. (Courtesy of Mary Ann Million.)

Leslie Elizabeth Ketter, daughter of Dorothy Million and Paul Ketter. (Courtesy of Mary Ann Million.)

Paul S. Ketter and wife Dorthy J. Million, daughter of Luther and Bessie (Daniel) Million. (Courtesy of Mary Ann Million.)

First row l-r: Clara (Million) Spencer, Hattie (Million) Nash; 2nd row: Jewel (Million) Click, Molinda (Million) Ratliff, Ada (Million) Shackelford, Mary (Million) Moss; 3rd row: Earl Million, Luther Million. (Courtesy of Mary Ann Million.)

Euphamy (Martin) Million. (Courtesy of Mary Ann Million.)

Phillip Wesley Million and Texanna (Lee) Million. (Courtesy of Mary Ann Million.)

Front row: Sylvia (Million) Collett, Texanna (Lee) Million, baby on lap is Earl Million, P.W. Million, boy standing next to P.W. is Luther Million, Euphamy (Martin) Million, Tom Martin, Mary Ann (Atteberry) Martin; 2nd row: Clara (Million) Spencer, Molinda (Million) Ratliff, Hattie (Million) Nash, Ada (Million) Shackelford, Irena (Million) Adams, Mary (Million) Moss. (Courtesy of Mary Ann Million.)

Bottom row l-r: Molinda (Million) Ratliff, Ada (Million) Shackelford; top row l-r: Hattie (Million) Nash, Clara (Million) Spencer. (Courtesy of Mary Ann Million.)

Norma and Jake Shackelford. (Courtesy of Mary Ann Million.)

Joe and Bertha (Tipton) Daniel and grandchildren. (Courtesy of Dorthy Ketter.)

Hal and Ada (Million) Shackelford. (Courtesy of Dorthy Ketter.)

Nora (Justice) and Charlie Daniel. (Courtesy of Dorthy Ketter.)

Paul and Dorthy (Million) Ketter. (Courtesy of Dorthy Ketter.)

Alvis Million and Jewel (Million) Click. (Courtesy of Dorthy Ketter.)

85

Luther, Bessie (Daniel) Million. (Courtesy of Dorthy Ketter.)

Levi Sandy "Jack" Ratliff and Molinda Jane Million (Courtesy of Dorthy Ketter.)

l-r: Christy Moore, Tommy Moore, Janet Moore, Roy Wayne Hankins, Mary Ann (Moore) Million, Leo Hankins, Charles Moore and Pagel Hankins. (Photo Courtesy of Mary Ann Million.)

Tom and "Matt." Jonathan Tomas and Martha Pace Clayton. (Photo Courtesy of Clodell Davis.)

Melvin Moore. (Photo Courtesy of Mary Ann Million.)

Grandma Pace and six of her daughters: Nell Pace (Ice), Grace Pace (Oxford), Edna Etta Gaskill Pace, Dutch Pace (Lowe), Ruth Pace (Adams), Martha Pace (Clayton), Rene Pace (Elmore). (Photo Courtesy Clodell Davis.)

Odell and Cleo Graham, Christmas 1966. (Courtesy of Clodell Davis.)

front row: George Gatewood, Majorie Putman, Alvin Wood, Ronald Wood, Della Wood, Elsie Gatewood, Roy Gatewood, Ellie Gatewood, Mafie Martin, Maxine Bagby, Mary Dee Holden. (Courtesy of J.D. Martin.)

Bill and Kay Gullette. (Courtesy of Bill Gullette.)

Pam Gibson with sons and their children, Ashlie Gibson (on left) and Tejal Gibson - 1991. (Courtesy of Stephen Gibson.)

Charlie Gibson with two sons. (Courtesy of Stephen Gibson.)

Pam Gibson with two of her grand-children, Tyson and Tejal Gibson. (Courtesy of Stephen Gibson.)

Charlie and Pam Gibson with oldest son, Michael - 1968. (Courtesy of Stephen Gibson.)

John, Linda Gibson with Danny, Eddie, Jennifer. (Courtesy of Stephen Gibson.)

John Gibson Jr. and John Gibson Sr. at property in Iredell, TX. (Courtesy of Stephen Gibson.)

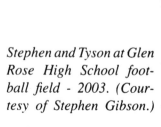

Stephen and Tyson at Glen Rose High School football field - 2003. (Courtesy of Stephen Gibson.)

John and Mildred Gibson. (Courtesy of Stephen Gibson.)

Stephen and Stephanie married on July 16, 1994 at Rainbow Baptist Church. (Courtesy of Stephen Gibson.)

Amos Alton Glass and Sarah Frances (Sallie) Hughes. (Courtesy of Joan Taylor.)

Mary Jane (Lafon) and William Glass. (Courtesy of Joan Taylor.)

Robert H. Shipman, Margarette Agnes "Sis" Glass - 1942. (Courtesy of Joan Taylor.)

William Glass, Mary Catherine Osborn, Lone Oak, Bosque, Glass County, TX. (Courtesy of Joan Taylor.)

James Cyrus Finley family.
(Courtesy of Luther Kelly.)

Christopher C. Rowland, Nannie
Emmaline Finley and family.
(Courtesy of Luther Kelly.)

Emma and Tabitha Gaither.
(Courtesy of Luther Kelly.)

Thomas C. Finley family. (Courtesy of Luther
Kelly.)

Nannie Finley Basham family. (Courtesy of Luther
Kelly.)

Thomas and Lucinda C. Finley. (Courtesy of
Luther Kelly.)

Front row: Burl and Della Rives; back row: Jack Rives, Flora Johnson, Mary Nelson, Pat Rives, Robert Rives. Laura Hensley didn't attend. (Courtesy of Billie Flanary.)

Jake Davis, Lillian Flanary, Ellen Tidwell, Bobbie Keller, J.M. Davis, Emma Ruth Nabors, Marvin Davis, Lucy Marchant. (Courtesy of Billie Flanary.)

Back row: Jerry Keller, Lynn Keller, Bobbie Keller, Ben Nabors, Emma Ruth Nabors, Ivan Davis, Lillian Flanary, Earl Flanary, Eddie Flanary, Billie Flanary; seated: Donald Ray Flanary, Nellie Flanary, unknown, Sadie Davis, Mattie Shackelford; on the floor: Tim Nabors, Donna Flanary, Cathy Keller. (Courtesy of Billie Flanary.)

Ivan Davis, Mattie Shackelford, Sadie Davis. (Courtesy of Billie Flanary.)

Tom Rives, Sam Rives, Burl Rives. (Courtesy of Billie Flanary.)

91

Family Reunion, Aug. 2, 1936, l-r: George Miller Shackelford, Henry Lee Shackelford, James Martin Shackelford. (Courtesy of Billie Flanary.)

l-r: Kaylee Flanary, Kirk May, Kelli May, Kyle May, Kara Flanary, Lindsey Flanary; on ground: Kevin May, Kathy May. (Courtesy of Billie Flanary.)

Billie Marilyn Rives, Loretta Louise Rives. (Courtesy of Billie Flanary.)

Jewel Russell with cousins May Bender and her sister Ruth Bender Hoff at Dinosaur Tracks in Glen Rose, 1940. (Courtesy of Russ Miller.)

William Glass family. (Courtesy of Joan Taylor.)

Joe Russell and Mary Russell with daughter Helen Russell at Stump Well. (Courtesy of Russ Miller.)

Art and Marie Studd. (Courtesy of Novella Wilson.)

Peggy Barnes. (Courtesy of Novella Wilson.)

Margie Powell with portrait. (Courtesy of Novella Wilson.)

Betty Black. (Courtesy of Novella Wilson.)

93

Margie Barnhill. (Courtesy of Novella Wilson.)

Naydean Davis. (Courtesy of Novella Wilson.)

Marlin and Fern (Wilson) Wood. (Courtesy of Novella Wilson.)

Back l-r: M.M. Bunt and Fronia "Charlie" Bunt - 1900. (Courtesy of David Barclay.)

Uncle of Little Joe Bunt. (Courtesy of David Barclay.)

Vada and Vernon Reynolds. (Courtesy of David Barclay.)

l-r: George Hankins, Julia (Moore) Hankins, Sonny Hankins, Walter Earl Hankins, Pagel Hankins, Leo Hankins, Roy Wayne Hankins, Donnal Hankins.

l-r: Doil Ray Moore, Della (Mann) Moore, Melvin Moore, Olvie Moore. (Photo Courtesy of Mary Ann Million.)

l-r: Julia (Moore) Hankins, Doris Faye (Moore) Phipps, Tommy Moore, Olvie Moore, Melvin Moore, Grady Moore and Vernon Moore - Oakdale Park - 1964. (Photo Courtesy of Mary Ann Million.)

Grady Moline Moore and Melvin Earl Moore, brothers. (Photo Courtesy of Mary Ann Million.)

Miller cousins, front l-r: Shirley Elliott Cooper, Barbara Ramsey, Linda Layne Branham; back: Billie Sue Elliott Vavloh, Neva Mimms Martin, Nancy Miller Moore, Connie Miller Scott. (Courtesy of Connie Scott.)

Wroten Henry Moore and wife, Addie Mae Whitworth, Oakdale Park - 1964. (Photo Courtesy of Mary Ann Million.)

Billy and Robena Miller. (Courtesy of Connie Scott.)

Jack and Susie Miller and family - 50th wedding anniversary; front l-r: Aleta Elliott, Susie and Jack Miller, Kenneth Miller; back l-r: Louise Dodson, W.C. Miller, Lella Mimms, A.D. Miller, Waldean Layne, Billy Miller. (Courtesy of Connie Scott.)

December 1960 - Jack and Susie Miller 50th anniversary. (Courtesy of Connie Scott.)

W.C. and Waples Miller, Katie and Nancy Moore - April 1986. (Courtesy of Connie Scott.)

Jack Erwin Miller, Susan Viola (Bunt) Miller. (Courtesy of Connie Scott.)

James Moss, Kathy (Smith) Moss. (Courtesy of Kathy Moss.)

L-r: Charlie and Lizzie 50th anniversary. James Moss, Lestine Moss, Mozelle DeMoss, Lizzie Moss, Dwane Moss. (Courtesy of Kathy Moss.)

97

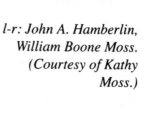

l-r: John A. Hamberlin, William Boone Moss. (Courtesy of Kathy Moss.)

Front, l-r: Charles Culburson Moss, Lalla Rooke (Hamberline) Moss, William Boone "Grandy" Moss. Back row: Maude May (Moss) Barclay, Myrah Fay (Moss) Trimble, Margrett Sue (Moss) (Davis) Miles. (Courtesy of Kathy Moss.)

George P. Milling. (Courtesy of Novella Wilson.)

Rebecca J. Lafon Hudson. (Courtesy of Joan Taylor.)

William Scott Lafon. (Courtesy of Joan Taylor.)

Beverly L. Lafon, son of William Lafon. (Courtesy of Joan Taylor.)

Mollie Lafon, wife of William Scott Lafon. (Courtesy of Joan Taylor.)

Lane family, l-r: Lee Lane, Ruby Lane, Linny Lane, Lanny Lane, Ann Lane Moss, Lorena Lane Hancock

Alva Kinsey, Margaret (West) Kinsey. (Courtesy of Rhonda Duffie.)

Helen Hubert, Ann and Sam Bluntzer, Helen Kerwin, Mark and Brooke Rollins, Scott Huburt, Zachary Hubert. (Courtesy of Helen Kerwin.)

Raymond King, Gladys King - 1954. Back row: Wayne, Bob, Gerald King; front: Jean King Nash, Ruth; bottom looking thru legs: Reta Ann. (Courtesy of Jean King Nash.)

Elmer and Eula King 50th anniversary. l-r: Juanita King Hooper, Donald King, Fern King Crews, Faye King McLemore, Jim King. (Courtesy of Jean King Nash.)

Back l-r: Fannie (Kelly) Reed, Eula (Jones) Kelly, Cyrus Kelly, Hazel (Kelly) LaLonde, Marie (Kelly) Barnard, P.J. Reed; front: Cap Kelly, Roy Kelly with dog, Nora with Jennie Kelly in front with Eddie in front of her, Barbara (Nora's daughter) and Marlie Barnard holding James. (Courtesy of Sammie and James Barnard.)

Standing l-r: Pete, Lee, Roy, Bill, Cap Kelly. Seated l-r: Jennie, Marie, Hazel. (Courtesy of Sammie Barnard.)

Cyrus Kelly, Eula (Jones) Kelly. (Courtesy of Sammie Barnard.)

Marie Kelly Barnard, James and William F. Kelly - 1946. (Courtesy of Sammie Barnard.)

Cyrus, Bill, Pete Kelly at Georges Creek ranch house - 1944. (Courtesy of Sammie Barnard.)

Sid and Audie Hopson, Jud LaLonde and Marie Kelly. (Courtesy of Sammie Barnard.)

Marie Kelly, Hazel Kelly. (Courtesy of Sammie Barnard.)

Hattie (Jones) Speigel. Photo taken at the home of Cyrus and Eula Kelly on Wheeler Branch. (Courtesy of Sammie Barnard.)

Raymond Elliott, Earl Elliott, Harmon Elliott. (Courtesy of Sammie Barnard.)

William "Bill" F. Kelly. (Courtesy of Sammie Barnard.)

101

Jennie (Finley) Kelly. (Courtesy of Luther Kelly.)

Washington Truman Kelly. (Courtesy of Luther Kelly.)

Hazel Kelly. (Courtesy of Sammie Barnard.)

Standing l-r: William Cyrus Kelly, Oscar Sinclair Kelly, Morgan Curtis Wade (a step brother), Luther H. Kelly, Arthur Franklin "Jack" Kelly. Seated: Franklin John Chamblee, their uncle. (Courtesy of Luther Kelly.)

William Rosea Kelly. (Courtesy of Luther Kelly.)

The Hudson family. Bottom row: Claude A. Hudson Sr., _, Albert "Dock" Hudson; back row: Gladys Hudson, Alvin D. Hudson holding son Eugene, Bertha Amy Hudson, Jesse Allen Hudson. (Courtesy of Rhonda Duffie.)

Kelly Brothers: Oscar Sinclair Kelly, Arthur Franklin Kelly, William Cyrus Kelly, Luther Horace Kelly. (Courtesy of Luther Kelly.)

Kelly Sisters. (Courtesy of Luther Kelly.)

Paul Hatler, Lillian Mae (West) Hatler, Willie Ruth Hatler Bradley. (Courtesy of Rhonda Duffie.)

Whitt family. Back row l-r: Dannette, Becky; front: Clinton Earl, Jayn and Wynell. (Courtesy of Becky Ice.)

103

Callie (West) Gardner. (Courtesy of Rhonda Duffie.)

l-r: Ben King, Alice Frances (Day) Hudson, George Washington "Wash" Hudson, Mrs. Kelley. (Courtesy of Rhonda Duffie.)

Walter Clark Gardner. (Courtesy of Rhonda Duffie.)

Callie West Gardner and children Walter D., Edwin J. and Toby. (Courtesy of Rhonda Duffie.)

Juanita Hulsey Willey. (Courtesy of Walter Maynard.)

Carroll and Rosa Lee Wilburn Hulsey. (Courtesy of Walter Maynard and Johnny Martin.)

Jimmy and Norma Stewart Hulsey. (Courtesy of Walter Maynard.)

David and Dora Hopson. (Courtesy of Dorothy Cox.)

Raymond and Ruby Hulsey. (Courtesy of Johnny Martin.)

C.A. Hulsey and daughters, Charlene and Verna Irene. (Courtesy of Johnny Martin.)

Charles Anderson Hulsey, Ivy Mae (Beasley) Hulsey. (Courtesy of Johnny Martin.)

Barbara Rebecca (Anderson) Hulsey, wife of John Henry Hulsey. (Courtesy of Johnny Martin.)

Leander Benson Howard, Mary Elizabeth (Renner) Howard. (Courtesy of Maxine Chadick and Lerlene Cullum.)

Mildred (Howard) Green, Willie Green. (Courtesy of Maxine Chadick and Lerlene Cullum.)

W. Frank Howard, Sallie Syrus Howard. (Courtesy of Maxine Chadick and Lerlene Cullum.)

Frank Howards store at Cross Roads. Grandchildren: Garland Howard, Johnnie Howard, Faye Howard, Glen Howard, Dugan Howard and Bobby Howard. (Courtesy of Maxine Chadick and Lerlene Cullum.)

Belle and Tobb Gatewood. (Courtesy of Maxine Chadick and Lerlene Cullum.)

Ethel Howard Black Ballard McCoy, Gracie Howard Martin Williams, Norman Howard, Johnnie Franklin Howard, Mildred Howard Green. (Courtesy of Maxine Bagby.

Harrison and Patsy West Hewlett with Lisa, Jan and Vivian. (Courtesy of Nan Sanders.)

Wesley House family. Back l-r: Denton, Dawson, Vivian, Bascom; front: Wesley, Lila, Annie. (Courtesy of Nan Sanders.)

107

Five Generations. John A. and Sue (Givens) Hamberlin, Florence Knight, Della Davis, Pauline Bone, Paul Bone (baby). (Courtesy of Kathy Moss.)

John A. Hamberlin family. (Courtesy of Kathy Moss.)

John and Mandy Goldsmith family. (Courtesy of Sammie Barnard.)

l-r: J.L. Adams, Virgie Lee Clayton Gaskill, Robbie Gaskill (child), Leola Faye Bohannon Moss. (Courtesy of Robbie Cummings.)

l-r: Robbie (Gaskill) Cummings, Virgie Sifford, Wanda (Gaskill) Barclay, Larry Sifford. (Courtesy of Rhonda Duffie.)

Robert Lee Adams came from Virginia and Margaret (Carrington) Adams. 771 b

Jesse Ruben Clayton, Mary Isabell Stacy. (Courtesy of Clodell Davis.)

l-r: Sonny Swaim, Mozell Swaim, S.L. Mann, Joy Bell Martin, Dutch Mann. (Photo Courtesy of Mary Ann Million.)

Tommy Brooks, Joy Bell (Martin) and Donna (Brooks) Lewellen. (Photo Courtesy of Mary Ann Million.)

Buck Martin and wife Bethel (Mann) Martin, daughter of Proctor Mann and Alice Row. (Photo Courtesy of Mary Ann Million.)

Martin family. Sitting l-r: Joy Bell, Jo Ann, Janice "Bob," Johnny and Janette; standing: Beth (Mann) Martin and Buck Martin. (Photo Courtesy of Mary Ann Million.)

Marvin Swaim, Linda (Mann) Swaim and girl in front is Mozell (Swaim) Tatum. (Photo Courtesy of Irene Mann Jolly.)

Linda (Mann) Swaim, daughter of Proctor Mann and Alice Row. (Photo Courtesy of Irene Mann Jolly.)

Carla Fenner and Bill Hodgekinson. (Photo Courtesy of Irene Mann Jolly.)

Lee Roy Hodgekinson and wife, Mary. (Photo Courtesy of Irene Mann Jolly.)

James McGraw and wife Nelda (Mann) McGraw. (Courtesy of Mary Ann Million.)

Elizabeth (Brown) Mann and Tommy Mann, son of Proctor Mann. (Courtesy of Mary Ann Million.)

Betty (Cornett) Mann and Thomas Kelly Mann. (Courtesy of Mary Ann Million.)

Jan (Mack) Mann and Tom Mann. (Courtesy of Mary Ann Million.)

Tommy Mann and dad, Tom Mann, son of Proctor Mann and Alice Row. (Courtesy of Mary Ann Million.)

111

Irene (Mann) Jolly, Lauren Riggen and Lori (McFall) Riggen. (Courtesy of Irene Mann

Ray McGuinn. (Courtesy of Irene Mann Jolly.)

Irene (Mann) Jolly. (Courtesy of Irene Mann Jolly.)

Lewis Howard, husband of Irene (Mann) Jolly. (Courtesy of Irene Mann Jolly.)

Shane, Gina and Rhiannon Sinclair. (Courtesy of Irene Mann Jolly.)

Danny, Mandi and Kade Thomas. (Courtesy of Irene Mann Jolly.)

Mandi, Kade Thomas and Raife Sparks. (Courtesy of Irene Mann Jolly.)

McFall family l-r: Lori, Carlyle, Elaine and Robert McFall. (Courtesy of Irene Mann Jolly.)

Back row l-r: Cecil Cook, S. L. Mann, Jake McFall and Emmett McFall; front: Tom Mann and Charlie Moss. (Courtesy of Irene Mann Jolly.)

Carlyle and Elaine McFall. (Courtesy of Irene Mann Jolly.)

113

Elaine (McCarty) McFall, Robert McFall, Carlyle McFall, Lori McFall. (Courtesy of Irene Mann Jolly.)

S.L. Mann and wife Carlene (Moore) (Bone) Mann. (Courtesy of Tracy Million Taylor.)

Robert Glen Mann, son of Silas Mann and Bonnie Swaim. (Courtesy of Tracy Million Taylor.)

Delyghte Britt Bullard. (Courtesy of Janell Gartrell.)

Gaylon Bullard. (Courtesy of Janell Gartrell.)

Back l-r: Wade Uptergrove and Justin Uptergrove; front: Jessie Uptergrove holding Sara Uptergrove and standing is Ashley Uptergrove. Jesse Gwen Bullard Uptergrove. (Courtesy of Janelle Gartrell.)

Lewis "Dutch" Mann, S.L. Mann, Bonnie (Swaim) Mann and Silas Mann. (Courtesy of Irene Mann Jolly.)

Seated: Clay Parker, Brenda Parker holding Bayleigh Marie Parker; standing: William Parker, Maridel Parker, Angela Michelle Parker. (Courtesy of Janelle Britt Gartrell.)

Gay Lynn Bullard. (Courtesy of Janelle Gartrell.)

l-r: Zach Parker and William Parker. (Courtesy of Janelle Britt Gartrell.)

l-r: Maridel Parker holding Austin William Parker, Bayleigh Marie Parker, William Parker. (Courtesy of Janelle Britt Gartrell.)

Jack Ramsey. (Courtesy of Betty J. Gosdin.)

Jay Ramsey, Jack and Pat Ramsey's son. (Courtesy of Betty J. Gosdin.)

Brenda Gartrell. (Courtesy of Janelle Britt Gartrell.)

Lisa Ramsey, Jack and Pat Ramsey's daughter. (Courtesy of Betty J. Gosdin.)

Pat and Mike Ramsey. (Courtesy of Betty J. Gosdin.)

116

Tom Mann and Jim Mann, sons of Proctor Mann and Jim Mann. (Courtesy of Mary Ann Million.)

Jim Mann and wife Dessie (Benton), son of Proctor Mann and Alice Row. (Courtesy of Mary Ann Million.)

Cecil Mann, son of Proctor Mann and Alice Row. (Courtesy of Tracy Million Taylor.)

l-r: Flora (Mann) Hamilton, Jim Mann, Dessie (Benton) Mann, Sandy (Reynolds) Mann, Lynn Mann. (Courtesy of Mary Ann Million.)

Jim Mann and Irene (Mann) Jolly, children of Proctor Mann and Alice Row. (Courtesy of Tracy Million Taylor.)

117

Back l-r: Cecil Mann, Ada (Joseph) Mann, Bill Tom, Carolin, Danny and Bob. (Courtesy of Tracy Million Taylor.)

l-r: Winton Gartrell, Earl Gartrell, Floyd Gartrell, Pauline Camp, Wanda Gartrell, Alpha Camp, Jane Gartrell. (Courtesy of Janelle Britt Gartrell.)

Janelle (Britt) Gartrell and Nora Gartrell. (Courtesy of Janelle Britt Gartrell.)

l-r: Nora Gartrell and Floyd Gartrell. (Courtesy of Janelle Britt Gartrell.)

l-r: Carol Gartrell Sturgeon, Brenda Parker, Deborah Gartrell, Laurie Gartrell Bryant. (Courtesy of Janelle Britt Gartrell.)

118

Norman "Red" Gartrell and Nora Gartrell. (Courtesy of Janelle Britt Gartrell.)

l-r: Geraldine, Dixie, Juanita and Tommy Donald Gosdin, children of Tom and Opal Gosdin. (Courtesy of Betty J. Gosdin.)

Thomas Barto "Tom" and Opal (Saunders) Gosdin. (Courtesy of Betty J. Gosdin.)

Marvin Dale Gosdin, son of Tom and Ruby (Hall) Gosdin. (Courtesy of Betty J. Gosdin.)

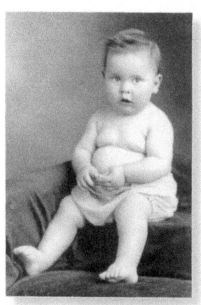

Sybol Gosdin. (Courtesy of Betty J. Gosdin.)

Sybol (Gosdin) McCoy. (Courtesy of Linda Beauchamp.)

Wanda McCoy. (Courtesy of Betty J. Gosdin.)

Jimmy Franklin McCoy (age 7), son of Sybol (Gosdin) McCoy and Cecil McCoy. (Courtesy of Betty J. Gosdin.)

Vern Gosdin. (Courtesy of Betty J. Gosdin.)

Carl and Peggy (Moore) Simmons. (Courtesy of Betty J. Gosdin.)

l-r: Lotus Gosdin, Vernon Gosdin and Mary Ruby Gosdin. Taken before the birth of Chester Ray Gosdin. (Courtesy of Betty J. Gosdin.)

Clarence and Ruby (Gosdin) Moore. (Courtesy of Betty J. Gosdin.)

Theodore Jackson Gosdin and Riley Franklin Gosdin Jr. (Courtesy of Red Gosdin.)

l-r: Larry Franklin Gosdin, Carol Jean (Gosdin) Gartrell, Kathy Marie Gosdin, Gary Wendell Gosdin. (Courtesy of Betty J. Gosdin.)

l-r: Lorene (Gosdin) Gilleland and Lois Marie (Hatcher) Gosdin. (Courtesy of Red Gosdin.)

Back row l-r: Sheila Ann (Locke) Gosdin, Larry Franklin Gosdin; front: Jennifer Ann, Angela Dawn and Melissa Marie. (Courtesy of Betty J. Gosdin.)

Lois Marie (Hatcher) and Riley Franklin Gosdin Jr. (Courtesy of Betty J. Gosdin.)

John Amos and Mary Virginia Vestor (Rape) Offutt. (Courtesy of Betty J. Gosdin.)

John Amos and Mary Virginia Vestor (Rape) Offutt and sons, Thomas and James Wayne Offutt. (Courtesy of Betty J. Gosdin.)

John Amos and Mary Virginia Vestor (Rape) Offutt and son, James Wayne "Jim" Offutt and wife Blanche (Groomer) and children. (Courtesy of Betty J. Gosdin.)

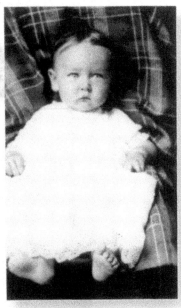

Thomas "Tom" Offutt. (Courtesy of Betty J. Gosdin.)

Offutt family reunion in 1938. (Courtesy of Dortha Beck and Peggy Huffman.)

Silas Scott Offutt and his horses. (Courtesy of Betty J. Gosdin.)

Silas Scott Offutt. (Courtesy of Betty J. Gosdin.)

Theodore Preston "Press" and Sue (Fullerton) (Gosdin) Offutt Jr. (Courtesy of Betty J. Gosdin.)

Theodore Preston "Press" Offutt Jr. (Courtesy of Betty J. Gosdin.)

William Theodore Offutt, son of Theodore Preston "Press" and Sue (Fullerton) (Gosdin) Offutt. (Courtesy of Peggy Huffman and Dortha Beck.)

Melba Beck and Bob White, May 6, 1967, Jr. and Sr. banquet. (Courtesy of Dortha Beck.)

Back: Robert Michael White, Melba Gail (Beck) White, Joey Glynn White; front: Jacki White and Jeremy Michael White. (Courtesy of Dortha Beck.)

Jim Daniel, son of William Daniel. (Courtesy of Betty J. Gosdin.)

The Daniel Family. Front: Joe Cephas Jr., Bertha (Tipton), Joe Cephas Sr.; back: Ollie, Howard, Charlie, Ruby, Myrtle, Willie, Bessie and Ethel Daniel. (Courtesy of Dorothy Ketter.)

l-r: Sadie (Nabors) Norman, J.B. "Wheeler" Nabors, Ben Nabors, Pearl (Nabors) Daniel. (Courtesy of Rhonda Duffie.)

Joshua "Josh" Offutt (left) and brother Theodore Preston Offutt Sr., sons of Thomas W. and Mary Jane (Pendley) Offutt. (Courtesy of Betty J. Gosdin.)

Gabriel Taylor "Gabe" and Mary Ann "Polly" (Smith) Daniel. (Courtesy of Betty J. Gosdin.)

Joshua "Josh" and Mary Elizabeth "Lizzie" (Hale) Offutt and daughter, Lilly Maud Offutt. Children not pictured are Dora Irene Offutt and William Gordon Offutt. (Courtesy of Betty J. Gosdin.)

Les, Opal, Pearl (girl) and Wallace (baby) Gosdin. (Courtesy of Betty J. Gosdin.)

Mildred Delilah (Garner) Ramsey and Doyle Ramsey and children: Elaine, Jack and Janice Ramsay. (Courtesy of Betty J. Gosdin.)

Wallace and Viola Gosdin. (Courtesy of Betty J. Gosdin.)

Grandchildren of Caroline (Ramsey) Dykes: Adam, Zachariah, Nick and Zachary. (Courtesy of Betty J. Gosdin.)

Randy Green and wife Ella (Rhodes) (Green) Sartor and Leonard Green at Oden. (Courtesy of Betty J. Gosdin.)

l-r: Robert Dykes and wife Michelle, Caroline (Ramsey) Dykes and boys, Adam and Nick. (Courtesy of Betty J. Gosdin.)

Theodore and Margaret Rose (Whitson) Offutt family. Back row (boys), l-r: Silas Scott "Sy" Offutt, George Howard Offutt, Theodore Preston "Press" Offutt Jr.; seated: Rosa Delia Offutt (age 5), Theodore Preston Offutt Sr., Margaret Rose (Whitson) Offutt and Willie Offutt. (Courtesy of Betty J. Gosdin.)

Cassie Jewel Offutt. (Courtesy of Betty J. Gosdin.)

Terry, Robin and Jacob Gosdin. (Courtesy of Red Gosdin.)

February 1962, l-r: Pamela Kaye Huffman, Melba Gail Beck and Danny Dale Beck. (Courtesy of Dortha Beck.)

Danny Dale Beck. (Courtesy of Dortha Beck.)

Dortha Margaret (Odom) Beck, Hubert Bartley Beck and Melba Gail Beck. (Courtesy of Dortha Beck.)

Rebecca Jane "Becky" (Gosdin)Daniel.(Courtesy of Betty J. Gosdin.)

l-r: Hunter Gass, Ferrell Gass, Tad Gass and Kimberly Jo (Huffman) Gass. (Courtesy of Peggy Huffman.)

Ezekiel Price "Zeke" Daniel, age 91, with great-grandson - Brea, CA. (Courtesy of Betty J. Gosdin.)

Emma Daniel. (Courtesy of Betty J. Gosdin.)

Top to bottom: Louise Berry and Helen (Moseley) Newkirk. (Courtesy of Betty J. Gosdin.)

Emily Caroline Gosdin and Garrett Lynn Gosdin. (Courtesy of Betty J. Gosdin.)

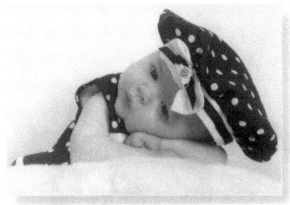

Mary Elizabeth Gosdin. Daughter of Bradly Eric and Ann Marie (Luckstead) Gosdin. (Courtesy of Betty J. Gosdin.)

Helen Newkirk. (Courtesy of Betty J. Gosdin.)

Back l-r: Lorraine Kay (Jasnocha) Gosdin, Bradly Eric "Brad" Gosdin, Brian Craig Gosdin; front: Tommy Lynn "Tom" Gosdin, Betty Jean (Wardlow) (Marietta) Gosdin and Garrett Lynn Gosdin. (Courtesy of Betty J. Gosdin.)

Bradly Eric "Brad" Gosdin and Ann Marie (Luckstead) Gosdin. (Courtesy of Betty J. Gosdin.)

In memory of Kathleen "Kit" Michaels best friend of Betty J. Gosdin, 1937-97. (Courtesy of Betty J. Gosdin.)

Four generations: Sarah Elizabeth (Scruggs) Gilleland, Maude Elizabeth (Gilleland) Martin, Anna Mae (Martin) Rich, Barbara Ann (Rich) Vermillion. (Courtesy of Betty J. Gosdin.)

Shane, Pamela Kay (Fox) and Tom Kammerer. (Courtesy of Betty J. Gosdin.)

Janie, Pauline, Anne, Jerry, Jack, Dub, Mary and Jesse Gilleland (1964). (Courtesy of Lorene Gilleland.)

Andrew, Debbie and Glen Fox. (Courtesy of Betty J. Gosdin.)

Back l-r: Earl Monroe Fox, Willie Lucille (Gosdin) Fox, Pamela Kay "Pam" Fox, Glen Fox. (Courtesy of Betty J. Gosdin.)

Terry and Theresa Gosdin. (Courtesy of Red Gosdin.)

Theodore Jackson "Red" and Betty Louise (Plummer) Gosdin. (Courtesy of Red Gosdin.)

Ira Stanley Plummer and Attie J. (Hawkins) Plummer. (Courtesy of Red Gosdin.)

131

Back l-r: Robert White, Lonny Parsons, Joe Earl Huffman, Ferrell Gass, Ronnie Beck, Melba (Beck) White, Dortha (Odom) Beck, Peggy (Odom) Huffman; middle: Jeremy White, Diana Parsons, Cassie Jewel (Offutt) Odom, Hunter Gass, Kimberly Jo (Huffman) Gass, Pamela Kaye (Huffman) Parsons; seated in front: Randy Joe Parsons, Tad Gass, Cassie Beck and Jacki White. (Courtesy of Peggy Huffman.)

Riley Franklin Gosdin Sr. and Susan Elizabeth "Susie" (Fullerton) Gosdin. (Courtesy of Betty J. Gosdin.)

Travis Odom. (Courtesy of Dortha Beck and Peggy Huffman.)

Tom and Bonnie Odom. (Courtesy of Peggy Huffman and Dortha Beck.)

l-r: Theresa (Gosdin) Trimble, baby Benjamin "Ben" Trimble, Sammy Trimble, Wendy Trimble. (Courtesy of Red Gosdin.)

Back row l-r: Cassie Jewell (Offutt) Odom, Dortha Margaret (Odom) Beck; front: Peggy Jewel (Odom) Huffman and Bernice Alton Odom. (Courtesy of Dortha Beck and Peggy Huffman.)

Theodore Preston Offutt Sr. and Peggy Jewel (Odom) Huffman - October 1939. (Courtesy Peggy Huffman.)

Jim and Kathy Gosdin. (Courtesy of Kathy Gosdin.)

Ezekiel Henry "Jack" and Beatrice Frances "Bea" (Daniel) Gosdin. (Courtesy of Betty J. Gosdin.)

Back l-r: Garrett Lynn Gosdin, Brian Craig Gosdin; front: Emily Caroline Gosdin, Lorraine Kay "Lori" (Jasnocha) Gosdin. (Courtesy of Betty J. Gosdin.)

133

Tamara Ranee "Tammy" Gosdin, 5 years old. (Courtesy of Betty J. Gosdin.)

Kristi Loree Gosdin, October 1990. (Courtesy of Betty J. Gosdin.)

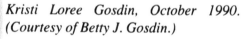

Paw Carter with Tony Gosdin. (Courtesy of Kathy Gosdin.)

James Anthony "Tony" Gosdin, October 1990. (Courtesy of Betty J. Gosdin.)

Sibyleen R. (Rhodes) Jackson and Swan Jackson. (Courtesy of Betty J. Gosdin.)

134

l-r: Lee Lawley, Ellen Lawley and Elaine Lawley. (Courtesy of Betty J. Gosdin.)

Billy Jean Rhodes, Annie Mae (Privitt) Rhodes, Charles Emerson Rhodes and Sibyleen Rhodes. (Courtesy of Nancy Moore.)

Martin A. Rhodes, Sylvia Lee (Whittington) Rhodes, Johnnie Ruth and Mary Margaret Rhodes. (Courtesy of Betty J. Gosdin.)

Janice (Ramsey) Johnson and grandbaby, Jessie. (Courtesy of Betty J. Gosdin.)

Martin A. and Sylvia Lee (Whittington) Rhodes with son, James "Jimmy" Rhodes. (Courtesy of Betty J. Gosdin.)

135

Eva (Kelly) and Alvin Mann, son of Proctor Mann and Alice Row. (Courtesy of Mary Ann Million.)

Proctor Mann and Alice (Row) Mann. (Courtesy of Irene (Mann) Jolly.)

Mada McCoy. (Courtesy of Irene (Mann) Jolly.)

Sharla Gartrell, Winton Gartrell, Louise (Moore) Gartrell. (Courtesy of Mary Ann Million.)

Ozella (Tackett) Mann and Hager Mann, son of Proctor Mann and Alice Row. (Courtesy of Mary Ann Million.)

Standing l-r: Jeffery Gartrell, Jason Sanchez and sitting is Deborah Gartrell. (Courtesy of Janelle (Britt) Gartrell.)

Standing back row l-r: Bob Behan and Kevin Behan; sitting in front: Bob Behan Sr., Evelyn Behan and Tonya Jo Sebastian. Evelyn Britt Behan. (Courtesy of Janelle (Britt) Gartrell.)

Mary Ann (Moore) (Courtesy of Million. Mary Ann Million.)

David and Laurie Gartrell Bryant. (Courtesy of Janelle (Britt) Gartrell.)

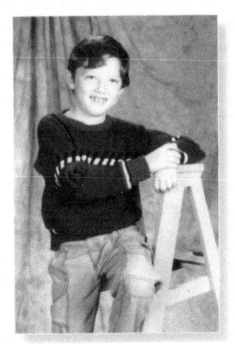

Michael Gartrell. (Courtesy of Janelle (Britt) Gartrell.)

137

Cody Daniel Bryant. (Courtesy of Janelle (Britt) Gartrell.)

Bonnie Britt Chapman and Lori Chapman. (Courtesy of Janelle (Britt) Gartrell.)

Larry Chapman and Bonnie Britt Chapman. (Courtesy of Janelle (Britt) Gartrell.)

Back row l-r: Doug Howerton, Blanche Britt Howerton; front: Shelly, Danny and Suzanne Howerton. (Courtesy of Janelle (Britt) Gartrell.)

Top row l-r: Delyghte and Blanche Britt; middle is Bonnie Britt and bottom is Bobbie and Dalton Britt. (Courtesy of Janelle (Britt) Gartrell.)

l-r: John Henry Britt Sr., Floyd Gartrell, Doug Howerton with Danny Howerton, Stanley Britt and Alvin Johnson. (Courtesy of Janelle (Britt) Gartrell.)

Charles Stanley Britt and Willie Britt (Courtesy of Janelle (Britt) Gartrell.)

l-r: Evelyn, Bonnie, Madeline and Janelle Britt. (Courtesy of Janelle (Britt) Gartrell.)

John Henry Britt Sr. and Dessie Sue (Chandler) Britt. (Courtesy of Janelle (Britt) Gartrell.)

John Henry Britt Jr. and Flora Britt. (Courtesy of Janelle (Britt) Gartrell.)

Front l-r: John Kirkpatrick and Allen Kirkpartick; back is Vickie Kirkpatrick. (Courtesy of Janelle (Britt) Gartrell.)

Back l-r: John Henry Britt Sr., Obe Britt, Reuben Britt; seated in front is Joel Huey Britt. (Courtesy of Janelle (Britt) Gartrell.)

Ida Britt and Rueben Britt. (Courtesy of Janelle (Britt) Gartrell.)

Dovie Britt and John Henry Britt Sr. (Courtesy of Janelle (Britt) Gartrell.)

Dott Stanley Britt and Evelyn Dase. (Courtesy of Janelle (Britt) Gartrell.)

l-r: Theodore Martin "Dock" Rhodes, Ruthie Mae Rhodes, Mary Ellen (Harmison) Rhodes. (Courtesy of Betty J. Gosdin.)

Front l-r: Emerson Rhodes, Matilda Jane (Roney) Rhodes (picture), Sallie Rhodes, Theodore Martin "Dock" Rhodes; back: Margaret, James, William and Minnie. (Courtesy of Betty J. Gosdin.)

l-r: Jimmy Helms, Larry Sikes, Vicki (Garner) Helms, Willie Mae (Rice) Garner, Amber Helms, Darrell Elwin Garner; front: Amy Helms and Kayla Sikes. Two are unknown. (Courtesy of Betty J. Gosdin.)

John Conover Harmison with grandson, Charles Emerson Rhodes. (Courtesy of Betty J. Gosdin.)

John and Minnie (Wiggins) Rhodes and children. (Courtesy of Betty J. Gosdin.)

Darrell Elwin, Willie Mae (Rice) Garner, Glenda and Gay Garner (baby). (Courtesy of Nancy Moore.)

Nancy Ellen (Garner) Moore and Elaine Ramsey. (Courtesy of Betty J. Gosdin.)

Pearl (Rhodes) Garner and Anthony Walter "Tony" Garner. (Courtesy of Betty J. Gosdin.)

Veda Loree (Garner) Gosdin and her grandchildren. Back l-r: Bradly Eric "Brad" Gosdin, Chad Shipman; middle: Kristie Loree Gosdin, Tamara R. "Tami" Gosdin, Veda Loree (Garner) Gosdin, Stephanie Nicole Shipman and Brian Craig Gosdin; front: Emily Caroline Gosdin, Garrett Lynn Gosdin, Anthony Walter "Tony" Gosdin. (Courtesy of Betty J. Gosdin.)

Back, l-r: Tom L. Gosdin, James Walter "Jim" Gosdin, William Arvil "Willie" Shipman; 2nd row: Betty J. (Marietta) Gosdin, Kathy Jean (Carter) Gosdin, Brian Craig Gosdin, Judy Darlene (Gosdin) Shipman; 3rd row: Veda Loree (Garner) Gosdin, J.B. Gosdin, Bradly Eric "Brad" Gosdin; front row: Tamara Ranee Gosdin, Stephanie Nicole Shipman and William "Chad" Shipman. (Courtesy of Betty J. Gosdin.)

Floyd Garrett and Lizzie Offutt and sons: Floyd Garrett Jr., Bud and Tince Offutt. (Courtesy of Betty J. Gosdin.)

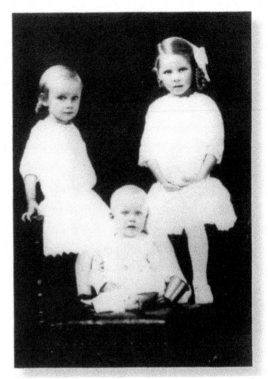

Pearl, Ellie and Bud Offutt. (Courtesy of Betty J. Gosdin.)

William and Donna Ice. (Courtesy of Nancy Moore.)

Nancy Ellen (Garner) Moore and William Moore. (Courtesy of Nancy Moore.)

Back: Sam Freas; front l-r: Richard, Melissa Loree "Missy" (Ice) and George Freas. (Courtesy of George Freas.)

143

J.L. Ice family. Back row: Sam, Jerry, Missy and George; front: Amy, Kevin, Richard and Donna. (Courtesy of George Freas.)

l-r: James Mann, Juanita Pritchett, Gerldine Fox, Freda Fox, Theodore Gosdin; front: Wendle Fox.

Ida Saxton, wife of President William McKinley, and daughter of James Asbury and Katherine (DeVault) Saxton and first cousin to Margaret Caroline (DaVault) Weston. (Courtesy of Betty J. Gosdin.)

Ola Irene Paris, wife of Esker Paris and grandmother of Ruth Cheek. Ola (b. Oct. 22, 1895, d. Feb. 23, 1956) and Esker (b. March 18, 1892, d. Nov. 4, 1952), both are buried Oak Grove Cemetery, Walnut Springs, TX. (Courtesy of Betty J. Gosdin.)

Girls from left: Lizzie Gosdin, Ruth Gilbreath, Laura Leonard, Delia Offutt, Ada; boys from left: Alf Leonard, George Offutt, Jim Gosdin, Ray Gilbreath. (Courtesy of Betty J. Gosdin.)

Blanche Mae (Roberts) (Sippy) Taplin and Harold Taplin, grandmother and step grandfather of Betty J. Gosdin. (Courtesy of Betty J. Gosdin.)

Blanche Mae (Roberts) Sippy and Lawrence Nelson Sippy, grandparents of Betty J. Gosdin. (Courtesy of Betty J. Gosdin.)

Back: Dorothy Mae (Sippy) Roye; middle: Jeanette Caroline (Sippy) Wheeler and Blanche Mae (Roberts) (Sippy) Taplin; front: Nathalie Audrey (Sippy) (Wardlow) Marietta (Courtesy of Betty J. Gosdin.)

Back, l-r: Robert Lawrence (Wardlow) Marietta, Betty Jean (Wardlow) Marietta, Kathy Cordelia Marietta; front: Robert George (Brueggemann) Marietta and Nathalie Audrey (Sippy) (Wardlow) Marietta. (Courtesy of Betty J. Gosdin.)

145

Ada Privitt. (Courtesy of Billy Jean Saffer.)

Will Privitt. (Courtesy of Billy Jean Saffer.)

Louise Privitt, Annie Mae (Privitt) Rhodes' baby sister. (Courtesy of Billy Jean Saffer.)

l-r: Charles Starling holding Morris, Teresa Starling, Jess Gilleland, Tony Garner holding Mildred, Mary Gilleland, Pearl Garner holding Veda, David Phillip Garner, Ritha Garner, Nancy Matilda Garner with children in front, Della (Knight) Garner (back), Zeb Garner, Nolan Moseley, Della (Shook) Garner holding _, Earl Moseley; four children in front l-r: Roy Garner, J.D. Garner, Pauline Garner, Helen Moseley - June 14, 1919 at old Garner place. (Courtesy of Paul Bone.)

Back l-r: Zeblin Thomas "Zeb" Garner, Ritha Delilah Garner, Anthony Walter "Tony" Garner, Arthur Augustus "Gus" Garner; front: Mary Frances Garner, Nancy Matilda (Weaver) Garner, David Phillip Garner and Teresa Tissue Garner. (Courtesy of Betty J. Gosdin.)

William and Birdie (Gosdin) Lambert and children: Lecia Pearl (b. 1907), Hubert Ray (b. 1910), Velma Mauzee (b. 1913), Oliver Hual (b. 1915), Ina Fay (b. 1918) and Lillian Alline (b. 1922). (Courtesy of Betty J. Gosdin.)

Lesley Courtney and Allie Opal (Bandy) Gosdin with Pearl and Wallace Gosdin. (Courtesy of Betty J. Gosdin.)

Eber Guy, Maide Eva and Oleta Annie, children of Wm. Pinkney and Clara (Gosdin) McDowell. (Courtesy of Betty J. Gosdin.)

Wm. Pinkney and Clara (Gosdin) McDowell. (Courtesy of Betty J. Gosdin.)

Roland Jackson and Nancy Amarintha (Gosdin) Heflin and children: Lum, Wilson, Kemp, Lucy, Vertress, Fannie, Ina and Mattie. (Courtesy of Betty J. Gosdin.)

l-r: Nettie, Stella and Edna Jones. (Courtesy of Mike Jones.)

Ezekiel Price and Lucy Ann (Harris) Gosdin and their 11 children. Top row l-r: Clara, John, Jim, Less, Becky, Jess, Birdie; bottom row: Bob, Nancy, E.P., Lucy, Sallie and Jack. (Courtesy of Betty J. Gosdin.)

Sarah Elizabeth (Turner) Powell. (Courtesy of Rhonda Duffie.)

Sam and Lily Jones. (Courtesy of Theda Deaver.)

Back: Harry Samuel Trimble, Bessie Fay Trimble; front: Milton Thomas Trimble, Sarah Jane (Bozorth) Trimble. (Courtesy of Dottie Hughes.)

Back: Cora Mae (Trimble) Chandler, William Leroy Trimble, Lester Clay Trimble, Nora Madge (Trimble) Lewis. Front: William Thomas Trimble, Ida Delia (Langwell) Trimble. (Courtesy of Dottie Hughes.)

Artie Louise (Wilson) Collings, Cecil Curtis Collings. (Courtesy of Novella Wilson.)

Back: Gary Wendel Tidwell (b. July 21, 1953); Ronald Eldon Tidwell (b. April 11, 1952, d. Nov. 7, 1989); Daphna Dell Standridge Tidwell (b. Feb. 14, 1932, d. Dec. 22, 1999); Eldon Wendel Tidwell (b. May 13, 1926); Sharon Rebecca Tidwell Hickman Pady (b. March 2, 1951); Michael Aaron Tidwell (b. Jan. 10, 1955, d. April 7, 1991). Front: Cynthia Beth Tidwell Johnson Stringer (b. March 15, 1957). (Courtesy of Eldon Tidwell.)

O.J. "Pop" and Margaret "Mag" Miles–1952 (Courtesy of Frances Hewlett.)

l-r: Jessie Geneva (Mathies) Arelleno, Pam Mathies, Cheryl Rosalie (Mathies) Canady, Alice B. Mathies, Jason Jerome Mathies. (Courtesy of Pam Mathies.)

Eric Weldon, grandson of J.D. Martin. (Courtesy of J.D. Martin.)

Laurie Martin Wallace, granddaughter of J.D. Martin. (Courtesy of J.D. Martin.)

Marc Martin, grandson of J.D. Martin. (Courtesy of J.D. Martin.)

Elizabeth A. Martin Blackney, granddaughter of J.D. Martin. (Courtesy of J.D. Martin.)

Lloyd and Jeannie Martin - November 2001. (Courtesy of J.D. Martin.)

Nann and J.D. Martin. (Courtesy of J.D. Martin.)

Mattie (Plummer) Martin, Charles Eugene Martin. (Courtesy of J.D. Martin.)

Clyde H. Bagby, Maxine (Martin) Bagby. (Courtesy of J.D. Martin.)

Buck Martin, Pearl Martin. (Courtesy of Johnny Martin.)

151

Back row l-r: Jeanette Martin, Brady Martin, Hope Martin; front: Hannah Martin, J.B. Martin. (Courtesy of Johnny Martin.)

Dennis Eldon "Buck" and Bethel (Mann) Martin. (Courtesy of Johnny Martin.)

Bill and Wilna Hackler Maynard, parents of Walter Maynard - December 1965. (Courtesy of Walter Maynard.)

Ken and Louann Nichols Maynard, Nathaniel Maynard, Stacy Rae Stuart, Amey Sue Stuart. (Courtesy of Walter Maynard.)

Amy Lynn Maynard, Texas Tech University, 1998. (Courtesy of Walter Maynard.)

Walter and Brenda Maynard. (Courtesy of Walter Maynard.)

Back l-r: Michael Johnson, Stacy (Taylor) Johnson, Vanessa (Ahlers) Taylor, Mathew Taylor; front l-r: Robert Taylor, Mary (Oates) Taylor, Lashae Johnson, (baby) Bailey Johnson. (Courtesy of Mary Taylor.)

Billy Joe Duffie and Rhonda Gayle (Mears) Duffie. (Courtesy of Rhonda Duffie.)

Back l-r: Kendra Lynn Daniel, Laressa Ann Daniel; front: Herman Jay Daniel, Laura Sue (Griffin) Daniel, Aaron Jay Daniel. (Courtesy of Laura Daniel.)

Mears Family. Back row l-r: Lois (Mears) Whitehead, Jack Mears, Emma (Mears) King, Lewis Jr. Mears, George Mears, Lizzie (Mears) Meek, Johnnie (Mears) Harkcom, Ruby (Mears) Johnston, Amos Mears, Mary (Mears) Copelin, Rosie (Mears) Hudson, Effie (Mears) Adams; front row: Ollie (Mears) King, Jesse "Short" Mears, Ethel (Hudson) Mears, S.L. Mears, Lee Mears. (Courtesy of Rhonda Duffie.)

Tell and Cordie Armstrong family. Back l-r: Sam White, Warren Eddy, Delbert and Emma Armstrong, Elva and Charlie Hackney, Coll Davis, Clyde Armstrong, Onen Nickels, Bill Armstrong; sitting: Juanita Armstrong White, Edith Eddy, Cordie Armstrong, Tell Armstrong, Lois Davis, Orlee Armstrong, Alice Armstrong Nickels, Mattie Dallas Armstrong, Gene Armstrong in Cordie's lap, Larry Davis in Tell's lap, Cordell (Davis) Wilson in Lois's lap, boy is John Tell Nickels. (Courtesy of Johnny Martin.)

Samuel J. Barr Armstrong, Martha A. (Little) Armstrong. (Courtesy of Johnny Martin.)

James Tell Armstrong, Cordie Cheek Armstrong. (Courtesy of Johnny Martin.)

Jessie Cox, Sarah Catherine (Murphy) Cox. (Courtesy of Theda Deaver.)

Samuel J. Cheek, Minerva (Farris) Cheek. (Courtesy of Johnny Martin.)

l-r: Jean Butler Echols, Miriam Wood Echols, Joe Don Echols, 1986. (Courtesy of Joe D. Echols.)

Covey family photo: Beth, Tim and Terry Covey about 1985. (Courtesy of Terry Covey, Granbury, TX.)

Clementine Fowler Echols, wife of Gordon Echols, on Sept. 15, 1886, Bell County, TX. (Courtesy of Joan Taylor.)

Albert Gordon Echols, son of J.L. and Laura West Echols, on Dec. 10, 1881, Somervell County, TX. (Courtesy of Joan Taylor.)

Ira Gordon Echols (son of Gordon Echols and Clementine) and wife Josephine Sudduth. (Courtesy of Joan Taylor.)

155

Janie Evans, Greg, David, Kevin and standing Joe Don Evans. (Courtesy of Carol Winters.)

Leona Eveline Ebert Evans, Robert Lee Evans, ca. 1960s. (Courtesy of Carol Winters.)

Beldon Maurice "Slue" English, Jennie Mae "Ginger" Statham English. (Courtesy of Ginger English.)

Joseph Carlton "Buster" Echols. (Courtesy of Joe Don Echols.)

Joan (Echols) Taylor, Pat (Echols) Simmons. (Courtesy of Joan Taylor.)

Standing l-r: Lance Simmons, Scott Simmons; seated: Robert Simmons, Pat (Echols) Simmons. (Courtesy of Pat Simmons.)

Robert C. Taylor, Bobbye Joan Echols Taylor. (Courtesy of Joan Taylor.)

Miriam Wood Echols. (Courtesy of Joe Don Echols.)

Doris (Adams) Eakin. (Courtesy of Doris Eakin.)

W.W. Nichols family. Back l-r: D.W. Nichols, William Jessie Nichols, Daisy Nichols, _, Seaborn Lomax Nichols, Homer Sherwood Nichols, Sears Richard Nichols, Roy Nichols, Ollie Brown Nichols, Jack Franklin Shipman, Guss Shipman, Archie Monroe Nichols, Dollie Sue Nichols (Palmer), Opal Nichols, Charlie Cooper, Ruby Zell Shipman, William Warren Nichols, Hilma Nichols, Mary Sue Cooper Nichols, Mamie Nichols Shipman, Hazel Shipman, Marshall Humphry Nichols. (Courtesy of Gusteen Jenkins.)

157

Phillip Buzan, Trish, Dylan, Deven. (Courtesy of Brenda Buzan Ransom.)

Brandi Buzan, Christian and Bryce. (Courtesy of Brenda Buzan Ransom.)

Gwen and Jerry Swink. (Courtesy of Aaron Judkins.)

James "Johnny" Martin and Marvilene Stewart Martin with Buck and Brady. (Courtesy of Walter Maynard.)

A.M. "Bill" Shook, Olen Shook, Herman Shook, Bynum T. Shook, Bercha Shook Underwood, _, Clyde Shook, Delia Shook Garner, Minnie Shook. (Courtesy of Faye Phears.)

Back: James Winters; front: Alex Winters, Carol Winters. (Courtesy of Carol Winters.)

Raymond Sanders family. Back row: Pat, Raymond, Kevin and Mike; middle: Ryan, Terry, Nan with Kaylee, Angela, Nathan; front: Matthew, Dacia, Jennifer, Brian. (Courtesy of Nan Sanders.)

l-r: Ila (Osborn) Stinson, Garland Osborn, Imogene (Osborn) Langdon, Anna Myrle (Osborn) Smith; sitting: Jerry Earl Osborn, Viola (West) Osborn, Marvin Osborn. (Courtesy of Kathy Moss.)

Kinnon D. Sandlin and Julie Irom Sandlin have four children; Ken Larsen and wife have three children; Doc Sandlin and Tobie Sandlin; Sam Love and Michell (Sandlin) Love have five children: Chandler, Cody, Carson, Samantha and Alyessa.

George Washington Powell Family (Photo Courtesy of Rhonda Duffie)

Lafayette "Fay" Powell and Rosa Powell (Photo Courtesy of Rhonda Duffie)

Bill and Lillie Powell, James Paxton Powell and Allen Hudson. (Photo Courtesy of Rhonda Duffie)

Bob Powell (Photos Courtesy of Rhonda Duffie)

Fonte (Powell) Beavers. (Photo Courtesy of Rhonda Duffie)

Joseph Emerson Shook and Minnie Florence (Bagby) Shook. (Photo Courtesy of Faye Phears)

Arvona Weaks Shook, Beulah Wilson Shook, Artie Smith Shook, Alan Underwood and Zeb Garner. (Photo Courtesy of Faye Phears)

Bynum Shook and Beulah Wilson Shook. (Photo Courtesy of Faye Phears)

John Amos Phears and Ila Faye Shook. (Photo Courtesy of Faye Phears)

161

William James West and Minnie Margaret (Haygood) West. (Photo Courtesy of Rhonda Duffie)

Robert Lee West and Mildred West. (Photo Courtesy of Rhonda Duffie)

Leon West. (Photo Courtesy of Leon West)

Jim Murray West and Lula West. (Photo Courtesy of Rhonda Duffie)

Mildred (West) Coleman and Hoyt West. (Photo Courtesy of Rhonda Duffie)

Hoyt West. (Photo Courtesy of Rhonda Duffie)

Mildred (West) Coleman. (Photo Courtesy of Rhonda Duffie)

Martha Jane "Eliza" (Sorey) West. (Photo Courtesy of Rhonda Duffie)

William James West, Eliza Margaret (Shields) West and Tommy West. (Photo Courtesy of Rhonda Duffie)

Robert Lee West Family. Faye, Annie, Ruby, Mae, Will, Robert and Margaret. (Photo Courtesy of Rhonda Duffie.)

Winnie Faye (West) Taylor, Annie Myrtle (West) Underwood and Lillian Mae (West) Hatler. (Photo Courtesy of Rhonda Duffie)

Notes

Notes

Notes

Notes

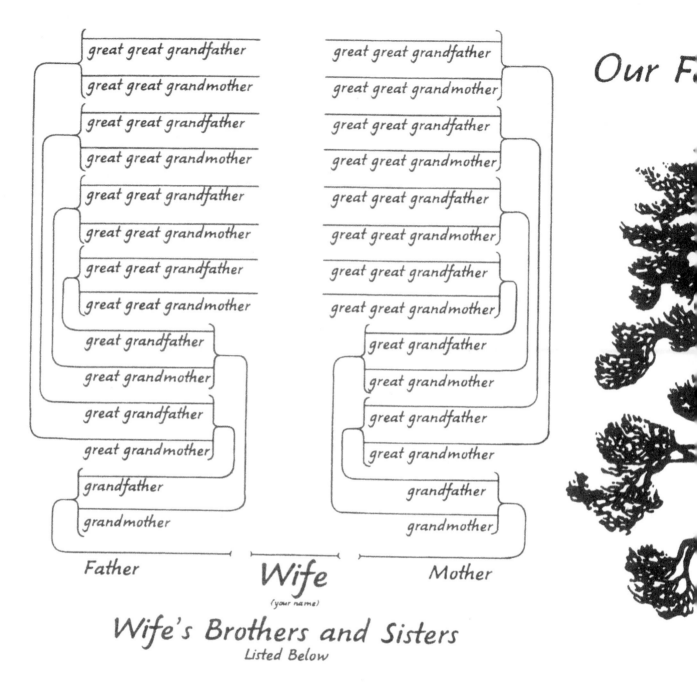

Our F

great great grandfather

great great grandmother

great great grandfather

great great grandmother

great great grandfather

great great grandmother

great great grandfather

great great grandmother

great great grandfather

great great grandmother

great great grandfather

great great grandmother

great great grandfather

great great grandmother

great great grandfather

great great grandmother

great grandfather

great grandmother

great grandfather

great grandmother

great grandfather

great grandmother

great grandfather

great grandmother

grandfather

grandmother

grandfather

grandmother

Father

Wife
(your name)

Mother

Wife's Brothers and Sisters
Listed Below

married to

children

married to

children

married to

children

married to

children

married to

married to

children

Our

married to

children

married to

children

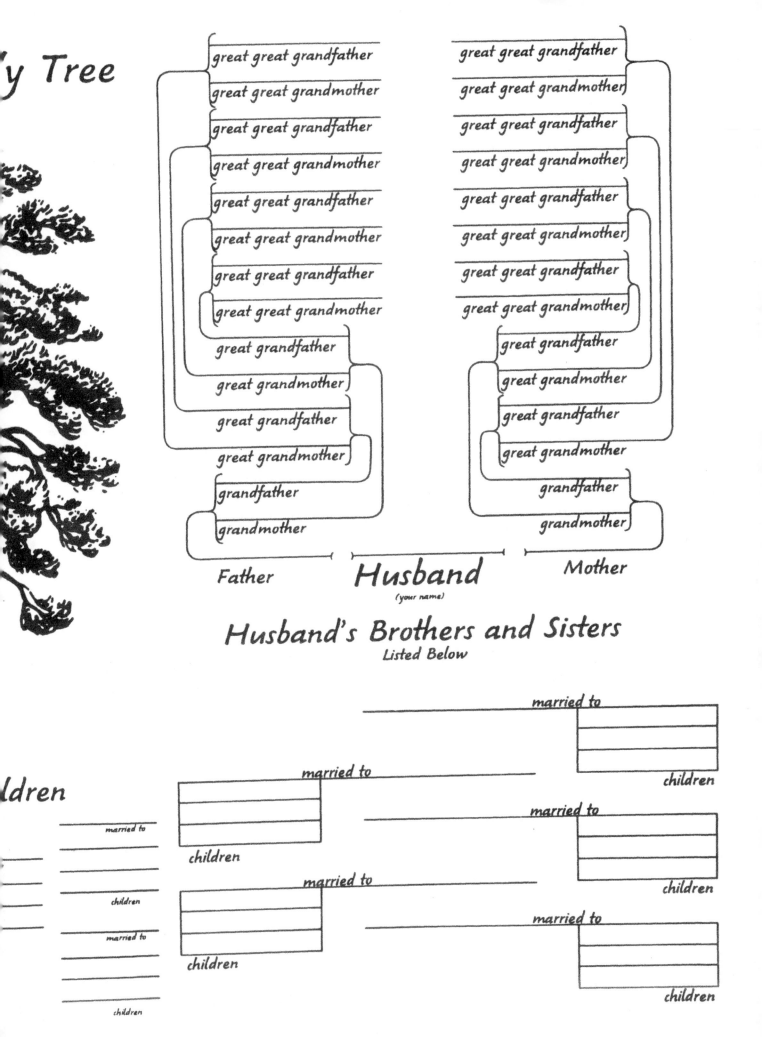

y Tree

great great grandfather

great great grandmother

great great grandfather

great great grandmother

great great grandfather

great great grandmother

great great grandfather

great great grandmother

great grandfather

great grandmother

great grandfather

great grandmother

grandfather

grandmother

great great grandfather

great great grandmother

great great grandfather

great great grandmother

great great grandfather

great great grandmother

great great grandfather

great great grandmother

great grandfather

great grandmother

great grandfather

great grandmother

grandfather

grandmother

Father

Husband
(your name)

Mother

Husband's Brothers and Sisters
Listed Below

married to

children

married to

children

married to

children

ldren

married to

children

married to

children

children

married to

children

Printed in the USA
CPSIA information can be obtained
at www.ICGtesting.com
JSHW060054150824
68134JS00032B/2729